How To Tur
Opportunities

ONE STEP AT A TIME

A 12-Step Journey with Inspiring
Stories to Empower Your Life

Marge Castillon Di Blasio

Copyright © 2019 Marge Di Blasio

All rights reserved. No part of this publication may be reproduced, distributed or transmitted in any form or by any means, including photocopying, recording, or other electronic or mechanical methods, without the prior written permission of the publisher, except in the case of brief quotations embodied in critical reviews and certain other non-commercial uses permitted by copyright law.

Although the author and publisher have made every effort to ensure that the information in this book was correct at press time, the author and publisher do not assume and hereby disclaim any liability to any party for any loss, damage, or disruption caused by errors or omissions, whether such errors or omissions result from negligence, accident, or any other cause.

Adherence to all applicable laws and regulations, including international, federal, state and local governing professional licensing, business practices, advertising, and all other aspects of doing business in the US, Canada or any other jurisdiction is the sole responsibility of the reader and consumer.

Neither the author nor the publisher assumes any responsibility or liability whatsoever on behalf of the consumer or reader of this material. Any perceived slight of any individual or organization is purely unintentional.

Cover Design by 100Covers.com
Interior Design by FormattedBooks.com

ISBN: 978-1-9991722-0-6 eBook
ISBN: 978-1-9991722-1-3 PaperBack

DOWNLOAD THE FREE RESOURCES

READ THIS FIRST

Thank you for investing in my book. As an appreciation, I'd love to give you a free gift.

TO DOWNLOAD, GO TO:

https://www.margediblasio.com/one-step-at-a-time-free-resources-su

DEDICATION

I would like to dedicate this book to the following people: My Mom, who taught me to be resilient and positive in life no matter what challenges I faced. Her life is a testimony of faith, hope and resilience. My husband, my biggest supporter. My kids, Arwen and Amelia, who have always been my inspiration. Someday, they will be old enough to read and understand this book, may it guide them on their journey.

To the ordinary people struggling to survive each day as they go through dark moments in life. May you continue to persevere, rise and keep moving forward as you inspire and share the blessings with others and live life to the fullest!

CONTENTS

Preface	ix
Chapter 1: Dare to Dream	1
Chapter 2: Find Your Burning Desire	14
Chapter 3: Make Decisions and Take Action	26
Chapter 4: The People You Meet Along the Way	42
Chapter 5: Delay is not Denial	47
Chapter 6: Let Go and Let God	56
Chapter 7: Forgiveness	60
Chapter 8: Be Ready to Receive	77
Chapter 9: Seasons of Life	82
Chapter 10: Giving Back to Others	89
Chapter 11: Achieving Your Goals and Setting New Ones	99
Chapter 12: Invest in Yourself	108
Conclusion	121
Acknowledgments	125
About the Author	129
Notes	131

PREFACE

The first step towards getting somewhere is to decide you're not going to stay where you are. – John Pierpont "J.P." Morgan

What if I told you I could share information that would inspire, encourage, and motivate you to take one step towards achieving a better life?

What if I said that, despite facing difficult times and struggling to survive, you could thrive?

What if you could discover the key to being unstoppable?

What if you could get what you want despite your present circumstances? Achieve your goals without compromising your values.

Would you be interested? Would you spend some time listening to me?

If you are tired of your current situation and have a strong desire to progress in life but are clueless of what to do, then you came to the right place.

One Step At A Time: How To Turn Your Adversities into Opportunities to Achieve A Better Life turns ordinary people, who are struggling to survive each day, into History Makers. People who make a difference, not only for themselves but also for the lives of others. The more you succeed in life, the more you can give.

One Step At A Time: How To Turn Your Adversities into Opportunities to Achieve A Better Life empowers survivors to break the cycle of pain and live to their full potential.

As you go through each page, with an open mind and open heart, prepare to be encouraged by real-life stories. Uncover the steps you can take, despite the darkest moments, that will lead you to a better life. A life that is available and waiting for you.

How to get the most out of this book?

This book is designed to encourage, inspire, and transform. It consists of twelve chapters that take you on a growth journey. It includes empowering stories about overcoming difficulties in life and provides the steppingstones to success. Each chapter includes insightful quotes from well-known people, ideas from experts on a particular topic, some strategies, and an "Over to you" section to help you test how you're doing. You will decide where you'd like to be, then find the support to take the actions required to get there.

The purpose of this book is to show you that, when you are aware of your options, you can turn your adversity into an opportunity. In my experience, when you are battling with a difficult situation, it is challenging to see a bigger world. In this book, you'll see life from a different perspective. You will learn to live a life with a higher purpose, despite the obstacles. You'll have the courage to take one step forward. You will be encouraged to continue investing in yourself, to live life to the fullest. You will stop focusing on your dark story and replace it with positivity. Your dark history has a great comeback story.

This book is not about judging anyone on the decisions they make, but to show that there are other ways to live. To thrive not just survive. If you allow yourself to follow the guidance and practical encouragement in these twelve chapters, nothing is impossible. You will recognize the importance of having options and that taking action will eventually get you there.

If you'd like some additional support, I've created free online downloadable materials that include all the forms and exercises in this book. Go to https://www.margediblasio.com/one-step-at-a-time-free-resources-su to download these bonus resources and find more information.

Remember, reading this book and being inspired is good, but what makes the difference is the action you will take. You must practice taking one step forward consistently, if you want to progress from where you are to where you want to be.

An effective way to see results is to team up with others. You can share what you've learned with your family, friends, or anyone you are connected to.

I wrote this book for you. I encourage you to take time to reflect on what you learn, do the exercises, and apply them in your life. Even if you have heard this before, it's how you follow through with what you've learned in each chapter that ultimately makes a difference in your life.

No matter how dark your situation is, you have the option to make things better. It is my privilege to share with you the steps that empowered myself and others to achieve a better life. Let's do it!

The origin of this book

It's been a while since I left my homeland and stepped into the unknown. When I left home, I also left abuse and a dysfunctional family, together with my comfort zone. I rarely think about it now, but every time in the past that I shared my story with others, I saw a spark in their eyes. I would briefly like to tell you how I decided to write this book for you and how it came into existence.

One day, not long after my twenty-second birthday, I woke up in the early hours and felt alarmed with the voices I heard. Screaming, yelling, and crying, the sounds echoed into my room. I saw my father and mother fighting. I had experienced this many times before, but this time, it felt very intense. I knew I had to do something.

"I can't continue living this way." This was the thought that kept playing in my head. I became obsessed with that thought. I realized, I didn't need to always live in survival mode. I didn't need to wait to get older, get a job, or find the perfect time to start progressing in life. I was astonished by the idea that, even though my circumstances were the same for a long time, I knew that better days were coming.

I faced trials and tempting situations that could have changed the path of my life, if I hadn't been clear about my values. I wasn't exactly clear on what to do, but one thing I knew for sure, I wanted to have a better life. A life, that when I had my own family, I would be proud to tell them of — an inspiration instead of one that causes trauma across generations.

I started to take one step at a time. Later, I realized that consistent action accelerated the journey of reaching my goals. My life got better and completely transformed.

First of all, I graduated with a Degree in Computer Science. Despite the challenges of surviving each day in my childhood, I made it. Second, I started many business ventures at an early age. Then, I became a youth leader. In my early twenties, I had lived in different countries, without depending on anybody, to support my family.

I flew my family to different countries and covered all their expenses. I explored the world of investing in real estate, the stock market, and online businesses. I became a licensed realtor, a certified John Maxwell coach, a writer, aside from being a grateful wife and mother of two beautiful girls.

The results of achievements attained, and blessings received, continued to flow to my family and others. The better life I thought impossible to achieve, wasn't as difficult to obtain as I imagined.

Later, I realized that dark moments in life don't determine one's destiny. I ultimately found healing from all the wounds in the past. I felt an authentic sense of achievement and clarity.

As I look back, I saw some of my friends and other people around me who had the same situation but never found ways to get better. They are stuck, and still surviving each day, not able to make a change. Wondering if there could be a helping hand that could come along and why other people like me got better — still believing that it's all about luck. People came up to me and said: "You've come a long way, you are lucky. Can you show me how to do it? How did you overcome your situation?" And I would say, "It's not luck. You have all the answers within you." That conversation later grew into the book you are reading right now.

Everything that I learned and discovered, the events that transformed my life dramatically, the steps I followed to share my blessings more to others – you are about to acquire in this book. As you keep your mind and heart open, as you go through each page, follow and embrace your journey. It will transform your life, your relationships with your family, friends, and other people around you.

I wrote this book for you.

MARGE CASTILLON DI BLASIO
Ontario, Canada

CHAPTER 1
DARE TO DREAM

Every great dream begins with a dreamer. Always remember, you have within you the strength, the patience, and the passion to reach for the stars to change the world.
− Harriet Tubman

Most people have a dream. Some of them, including myself, are willing to share it. Others want to keep it only to themselves. People often give up on their dreams, even before they get started.

Sometimes, you hesitate to make any move till you figure it all out. You decide to stay where you are because you can't predict how everything will unfold.

Early in life, you believe nothing is impossible and you dream big. But as time goes by, life gets more complicated and challenges arise. You lack the confidence to pursue your dreams. You get discouraged, stuck, and tend to give up.

Devastating heartbreak. Abuse. Poverty. Addiction. Depression. Death. Illness. Sudden changes. A life turned upside down, not knowing what to do next or where to go. It feels there's no way out. You've reached the lowest point of your life.

How do you get through dark times?
How do you break the cycle?

POWER OF A DREAM

A dream awakens your passion. It moves and inspires you. It allows you to imagine, without any limits, that you can be anybody you want to be. It gives purpose to your life.

In Put Your Dream to the Test, John C. Maxwell defines a dream as "an inspiring picture of the future that energizes your mind, will, and emotions, empowering you to do everything you can to achieve it."

You can't fulfill your purpose and grow toward your potential if you don't know where you should be going. You need to identify and sail towards your destination. In other words, you need to identify your dream. It all begins with a dream. Sounds simple, but it's the cold truth.

In Your RoadMap for Success, John Maxwell writes that each of us has a dream placed in our heart. A vision deep inside that speaks to the very soul. It's the thing we were born to do. It draws on our talents and gifts. A dream does many things for us:

- Gives us direction
- Increase our potential
- Helps us prioritize
- Adds value to our work
- Predicts our future

Let me introduce you to some dreamers. Ordinary people, who dare to dream, despite the darkest moments of their lives. Dreams that allowed their hearts to look forward to something bigger. Despite circumstances, adversities faced, they believed in the power of dreams.

A Child Loses her Mother

Virgie was eight when her mother had terminal leukemia. She

got separated from her abusive siblings and alcoholic father when her mother died. Her dream: "To bring my family together again and start all over."

"I love you. I'm sorry Mama has to leave…" Virgie's mom took a deep breath but did not inhale afterward. Nor did she blink, and Virgie's eyes dulled; she knew her mom passed away.

"Ma," Virgie pleaded, exhausted.

Virgie lost her mom at a very young age. She was the third child among the family of eleven children.

"In those last hours, I rested with her. I stroked her hair. I cried and told her I loved her. I kissed her cheeks. That last night is the beginning of the big change in my life," she said.

"My siblings and I took over doing the house chores. We fought daily over who would do the dishes and cleaning. My two eldest sisters won most of the time. I, being the third child, had to do everything for them. My father, drunk all the time, didn't know what was going on. One afternoon, I was running full speed down the field, when a metal object impacted my head. I suddenly crouched to the ground. I could feel the blood flowing. I saw my sister standing over me with an axe in her right hand, looking at me, furious as she caught me running around, playing, instead of doing the housework. I was in pain for a week after that."

She sobbed, "A few months after my mom's death, they diagnosed my eight-month-old baby twin sisters with pneumonia. I lost them too; then my grandparents adopted me. They spread out my siblings with my father and the rest of my relatives. I missed my family, my father, and my siblings; I had no clue where they were."

She paused for a while and exclaimed, "But growing up in the province, beside the deep blue sea, I had a simple dream. I wanted to move to a big city. Get a decent job and reunite with my family."

That dream became her inspiration and motivation. She saved enough money. She took the ferry to go to Manila, the capital of the Philippines, known as the land of opportunity. After six months, she connected with her eldest sister, Aurora, and planned to meet up.

"The moment my sister walked out of the airport, my heart sank as I remembered all that had happened. It's been 11 years since my mom died. Eleven years since we last saw each other," she expressed. But as she got closer to me and I hugged her, I felt elated. It brought back the happiness of being with my family again.

We sat on the table, talked, and planned to bring my father to the city to be with us. A year after that, my father was with us together with my siblings. It didn't happen overnight, but we made it happen."

A Boy's Life is Changed

At the age of six, Manny fell from the tree he was climbing. He developed stiff joints and a spinal disorder. An excessive outward curve of the spine resulted in an abnormal rounding of the upper back, also called hunchback. After the accident, he felt so alienated. His physical appearance had deteriorated so much. As a result, people taunted him, calling him "hunched, hideous, impotent."

He had a tough time when he was growing up. He felt insecure, rejected, and unworthy. Raised by a military dad, who died when he was in his twenties, Manny learned to protect himself by becoming a survivor. He faced his taunters in a tenacious and dominating way.

Despite his appearance and the ridicule that followed, he dared to dream about finishing his education, living normally and having his own family. Manny persevered; he completed a degree in engineering from one of the top universities, had a family, and managed a small business.

Don't allow your limitations to define you. If you accept what the world is telling you, all the limiting beliefs around you, then it will become your reality. You can go as far as your mind lets you.

"As you progress through the journey of achieving your dreams, you will be able to realize that the most difficult limitations and circumstances actually served as necessary tools that helped you become a better version of yourself."
- Amy Oraefo

One day, Manny visited his youngest sister at her home. He spotted an unfamiliar face babysitting his nieces; it was Virgie. Captivated by her beauty, he exclaimed, "I want to spend the rest of my life with her." That moment was the beginning of their journey as a couple. It was 1979 when they got married, moved into a small apartment, and built a new dream together.

Manny said, "My inspiration is my family. I wanted them to have a place to live, and food served every meal."

Virgie reckoned, "Quality Education. Once you have it, you have the confidence to speak up and a better chance to get an office job. Also, to grow up with both parents together."

The Realization of a Dream

I'm Virgie and Manny's second child in a family of four children. My mother, Virgie, used to work in a factory. When she had four kids, she struggled with the decision to return to work. She chose to be a stay-at-home mom.

Raising four kids was difficult with one income, but because my dad was working overseas gave us the option to live a better life than most. Mom wanted us to have the education she'd never gotten. She lost her mother when she was eight and didn't finish elementary school. As a result, she had limited work experience. She believed having a quality education would be a way for us to get a good white-collar job.

Eager to find other ways to make extra income, she explored different things. She converted the front of our house to a "sari-sari store," a convenience store found on almost every street corner in the Philippines.

Sari-Sari means "various kinds." It refers to a wide range of goods like candies, sugar, salt, coffee, detergent, soap, toothpaste, shampoo, cooking oil, canned goods, pop, beer, cigarettes, and many more selections. One of the unique things about it is how you can buy a singular item as needed. Instead of purchasing a bottle of shampoo, you can get a sachet for one or two. Mom was also a Tupperware consultant and an Avon representative.

When my eldest brother and I turned high school age, our expenses significantly increased. The profit she made from all her side hustles were not enough. She needed a steadier income while taking care of her four kids. With the blessing of my father, while he was working overseas, she converted half of our house to a canteen.

Living across the street from a university, beside a 7-Eleven store, we opened our small family restaurant. Every morning, she woke up at four o'clock and went to the market for a fresh selection of produce. By the time she came home, she had made sure our uniforms were ready and lunches were all packed. Then, she cooked and prepared breakfast for her customers before 7:00 a.m.

I helped with other chores before going to school. I cleaned the floor, prepared the tables, and washed the dishes. At seven o'clock, we had the students, faculty, and staff lined up, all excited to have their hot breakfast.

"Bye, Ma!" I whooped and kissed her cheek before I left. "It's a great day!" I cheered almost every morning. I was glad to see the customers enjoying the food and experience when I left.

It was a small family business, but being part of the process was like an internship for me. Customer service, hard work, patience, dedication, marketing, finance, and people skills, I felt thrilled to be part of it!

One evening, when my mom was planning for the next day, I asked, "How's the profit today, did we make lots?"

She replied, "just good enough to cover our budget for the next day's groceries."

"You started at 4:00 a.m. and closed late at night, Ma! You worked almost 16 hours a day, and that's all we got? Just enough to cover next day groceries." I asked, puzzled again with how long she worked and was not making more.

She nodded.

"That's just even then!" I questioned.

"Well, it covers the food for my four kids. You ate whatever you want, right? It gave you and your brothers the option to have an unlimited

meal for breakfast, snacks, lunch and dinner. I don't have to worry anymore for my kids' food. For that alone, it's all worth it," she stressed.

My hard-working parents were sacrificing their lives to give us a better future. Working longer hours, being sleep deprived, separated from each other, and giving up everything they had. Their sacrifice ultimately helped me find my dream. The financial freedom to provide more options for my family, meeting all our basic needs, and even enough so they could stop working if they wanted to.

Most successful people have hit rock bottom before climbing to the top. People with different stories, but what do they have in common? They started with a dream to change their lives.

Have you ever struggled to find time for your dreams?
Have you ever felt stuck? Can't find your motivation to keep the dream alive?
Have you gotten discouraged?
Have you given up on your dreams?

If you're struggling, my heart goes out to you. I've been there far too often. I understand the anguish and pain you're going through. I know what it feels like when your life turns upside down, not knowing what to do next or where to go.

Change is inevitable, and sometimes, life circumstances bring challenges. Remember that even though you may feel helpless, you're not. You are not alone.

Regardless of your circumstances, it's never too late to awaken that dream within you. It's YOU choosing to make things happen. You must decide because if you don't, someone else will. It's never too late to start.

Remember, every success story starts with a dream. It is a creative vision of your life. It gives you hope for today and to see the possibilities for the future.

Make time for what matters most to you. If it's something you want to pursue, it will grow with you and chase you wherever you go. Remember, **dreams that grow in your heart are worth taking a risk for.**

Take the first step. Dare to dream. Believe in your dream again. Once you believe, the courage will follow. You can do it — one step after another.

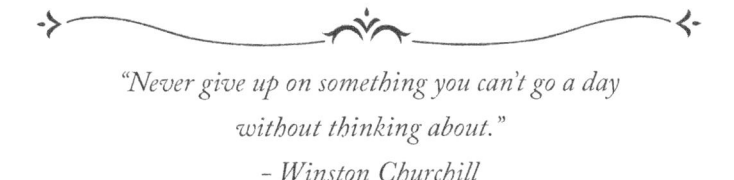

"Never give up on something you can't go a day without thinking about."
- Winston Churchill

"All your dreams can come true if you have the courage to pursue them."
-Walt Disney

Over to you:

The first step to get started is to have clarity about your dream. Start by searching inside your heart. Set aside a block of time to work through the following questions.

1. What is this one dream in your life that you want to achieve? Think of a dream that you could accomplish if you didn't have any limits or boundaries.

You may have one or many dreams. The goal is to identify them and have clarity. Remember: You don't need to know how you're going to make your dream happen; take the first step to identify it and write it down.

2. Why is this dream important to you?

Example: Write a book.
Why: I know there would be someone out there that could benefit and be encouraged by my story. Even if I'm no longer in this world, this will continue to reach out to others and will serve as my legacy.

It could also be vague for now.

Example: I want to have a better life.
Why: Because I would like to make sure my family has food to eat every meal and has their basic needs met.

3. What is so important to me that I would be willing to stay up all night for it?

If there is nothing that you can think of, It's okay. Don't quit. Give yourself some time to reflect. Meditate on the statement above and continue to ask yourself the guideline questions until you have the clarity before moving on the next chapter.

Look at the statement below. Examine what it will mean to you and take the first step. Identify your dream.

My dream is: _____
_____
_____
_____
_____
_____
_____

I recognize that turning my dream into reality is a process and not a destination. I commit myself to be successful. Life can get complicated. The road may get bumpy, but I will do what it takes to make this dream happen.

In later chapters, we will talk about what it will take to get you moving towards your dream. You're on your way!

CHAPTER 2
FIND YOUR BURNING DESIRE

Desire is the starting point of all achievement, not a hope, not a wish, but a keen pulsating desire which transcends everything.
– Napoleon Hill

Failure will never overtake me if my determination to succeed is strong enough.
– Og Mandino

What do you want out of life?
What is your heart's deepest desire?

Is it for financial freedom, vibrant health, a relationship, job promotion, self-mastery, business, travel, or to have a better life than what you have now?

Whatever your desire is, it is important to be aware of what you want in life. Without this continuous stream of desires, there would no longer be any reason to do anything. Life would grind to a halt, as it does for people who lose the ability to desire. An acute crisis of desire corresponds to boredom, and chronic depression.

Desires constantly arise in us. It is a strong want to have something or to make things happen. It is desire that moves us, and in moving us, gives our life direction and meaning.

Your Dream gets you started; your Desire will push you to move on to the next step.

How about in the midst of adversity? What is desire's role?
How would you pursue your dreams and desires if survival alone seems impossible?

We all face adversity from time-to-time. It is important to remember that even when you go through dark moments, you have a choice – to stay where you are, be in survival mode, or you can choose to explore, let go of limiting beliefs and doubts, by taking one step at a time.

No matter what your life circumstances are, if you desire to move forward towards your dream, change is important. Instead of thinking of the pain of change, think about the pain of staying where you are. You can achieve your dream if you have a strong desire to make it happen.

To get to the point where you want, you must be willing to take the first step of your journey. Take one step at a time and focus on the destination. Plan your next move. Then the next one. Each step contributes to your goal.

Be mindful not to get caught up in the planning stage, not progressing towards your desire. Remember, no one can guarantee what tomorrow will bring, but what you do today serves as a foundation for what you will achieve.

How we respond to adversity determines how resilient we can be when things go wrong. Here are some inspiring stories where, with an unyielding desire to live with a higher purpose, courage and resilience were born in the face of adversity.

Rising Above Adversity

One Sunday morning, around six, I was still asleep when there was a loud noise of a screaming man and a woman crying. I went into the living room and found my dad, holding his cigarette lighter, standing in front of my sobbing mom.

He shot her a venomous look and said, "I will burn you for accusing me!"

She looked him in the eyes and responded, "Accusing? Your kid saw you!"

His hands dropped to his sides to form clenched fists of tension.

Terrified of what could happen next, I took a deep breath and sprinted to my mother. Puzzled on what to do next, I paused, feeling inexplicably queasy.

"Don't dare to hurt her! I will call the police," I said in a croaky voice.

Boiling with fury, he ground his teeth and clenched his jaw so tight, it clearly hurt. He exploded, "I don't care," and walked away.

That moment was the beginning of my strong desire to pursue a better life, not only for myself but also for my family. The pain and suffering I'd seen in my mom motivated me to be focused on what I could do each day to thrive, not just survive.

It started with my dream. I saw what my parents had sacrificed to raise our family and to provide us a better life. I wanted to have the financial freedom to give them options, but my desire grew even stronger every time I experienced the pain.

I pushed myself to pursue side-hustles while I was in university. I had several part-time jobs related to my course. I provided computer repair and IT services and had built clients through referrals.

Living across from the school, I also started a computer center. With my parents' blessing, I converted a portion of our house to accommodate the business. I had a mentor, my high school instructor, who helped me find efficient ways to set up the center. I found a business partner, one of my close friends, who helped me expand. Aside from computer rentals, we provided other services — encoding, image editing, even teaching computer courses. The business was growing steadily. I was making good money for a side hustle. Most of all, I was growing, enjoying the process, and was unstoppable.

I grew up with a father working overseas in an oil firm, who came home for two weeks once a year. He was the financial provider in the family. While his sacrifice of working to provide for us is great, he missed out on the opportunity to cultivate a healthy relationship with his kids.

A year before I finished my degree, my father came back from his work overseas. His project got canceled. He got his severance and was thanked for his service.

The first few days I had him back together with my family felt good. We looked forward to learning from him since we had grown apart for years.

He focused on how my mom managed our rental properties. He also assessed how effective I was in my business. Since things were more stable than before in the computer center, he had me pay for the rent and the utility bills. I thought it was a reasonable request. I was excited. He wanted me to grow. I knew my responsibilities as an entrepreneur. So, I paid for the rented space, utility bills, and other costs associated with running the business.

Then one day, he introduced me to another tenant with a similar business, a computer center. He wanted me to share the space I used. He proposed that the profit would go to the computer that the customer used. I didn't like the idea and worked directly with the new tenant to split all the profit instead. We operated together in the business. After a year, I quit. Things get more complicated with me involved, and my father questioned what I gave back to them.

I realized, after my father lived with us again for a few months, that we were strangers to one another. As the days went by, the excitement we used to have to be with him around vanished. He questioned everything we did; there was no filter, no boundaries. It led to more tension in my family. He drank more often, yelled at everybody. He controlled and took over my life and my family.

I was young and had a dream but being in a dark place, I didn't know what to do nor where to go.

Insecurity and fear replaced the confidence I used to have. I felt defeated. But something held me back, the thought of having an ideal family. Divorce was uncommon at that time in the culture I came from. I was hoping for something that would restore the love and respect in my family. I tried to survive each day. If I could make it another day, maybe it would get better.

At one corner of my tiny little room, I poured out my tears. I prayed every day and night for the sorrow to disappear and to have a better life. But each day, as I stepped out of my room, nothing changed.

Instead of focusing on the situation, I set my eyes on positive things. Reminded myself that it would get better if I took one step at a time. Finally, one day, I realized, something inside of me was changing. I started to toughen up. My faith was rising; my focus shifted.

I exclaimed, "I have to change this for my family. My mom, who has given her entire life to raising me and my brothers deserves better than this. My siblings are still too young to grow up agonizing. "

It was no longer about my sorrow, insecurity, defeat, the toxic situation, anger, or a miserable life. It was no longer about me. I started to see things from a different perspective. No longer a Victim but as Creator and began living a life with a Higher Purpose. I focused on what I could do next. I explored the options I had.

At that time, I only saw two. First, to be a prostitute, a quick way to earn money, or second, finish school, and get a decent job.

In third world countries, prostitution is often a result of entrenched poverty. Using your body as a commodity requires no education, no references and no experience. Growing up, I have seen it in the media and knew people in my neighborhood and school involved with it.

For some, it was their choice, a quick way to make money. But there's another group that wanted to get out for a very long time but were beaten black and blue when they were caught. Someone decided for them and kept them a victim and they are seeking our help.

Although exposed to this environment, I chose my second option: to finish school and get a decent job. It's not that I've always known I would get a high paying job after school. It was just very clear to me from an early age to make a decision aligned with my values.

I give credit to my mom who helped me to shape my standards. Even when temptations surrounded me, I knew what to do, I never questioned nor compromised my values.

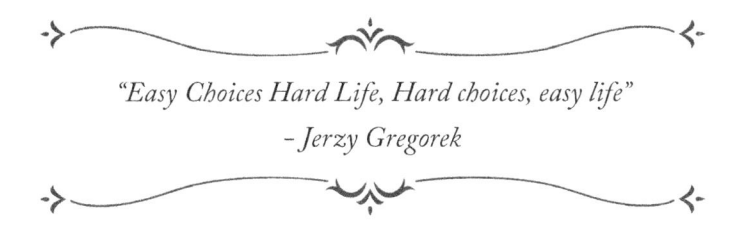

"Easy Choices Hard Life, Hard choices, easy life"
- Jerzy Gregorek

This decision led me to dream big. A strong desire to make a change, to have a better life. I may not have had the roadmap of what exactly I wanted to do but I was clear about one thing: To make a decision based on my values.

Once I decided that, I was able to proceed with the next step.

There are lots of unknowns, a mixture of excitement and fear but that makes the journey more interesting.

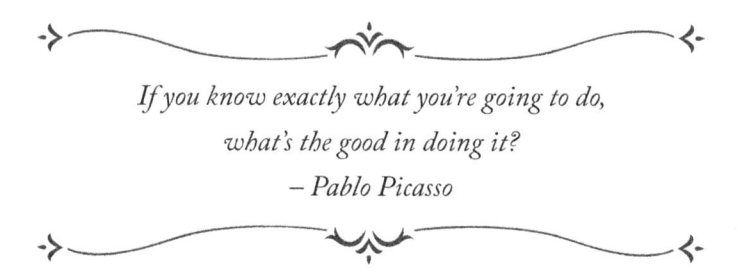

If you know exactly what you're going to do,
what's the good in doing it?
– Pablo Picasso

Every morning and night, I heard my mom flipping the pages of her bible, breathing deeply and settling in for her daily devotions with God. She never forced me to read it, but she lived by example. When she's was in agony, or when things went astray, she reflected on the word of God. When she was happy, relaxed, she also read it.

One evening, she said, "I was in my late twenties. Sleep deprived and exhausted when you and your brothers suffered from fever; then your dad comes home stoned."

He yelled, "F***k! Why are all the kids in bed!"

I replied, "All of them are sick, and this is the only way I can look after all of them."

Agitated, he shouted, "This is my house; take all of them."

With tears in her eyes, she said, "The physical and verbal abuse was excruciating. Until, one night, I slouched towards the front of the house, glum, hands thrust in my pockets. Noly was nine, Marvin was five, and you were seven, I was ambivalent about staying in this relationship and puzzled where to go. Exhausted with your father, I couldn't handle it anymore, all I wanted was to leave."

She had no mom, no dad, no siblings, no friends around. She didn't have any income nor savings. Her whole world seemed to be moving in slow motion. She felt like she was at the end of her rope.

Then she took a deep breath, and said, "Then I stared at you playing with your siblings, and you smiled back. I saw the angelic, innocent, and helpless kids I had. It brought back all the struggles I had when I grew up without my mom beside me, so I stood up and hugged the three of you. I told myself to get up. I decided to stay, toughen up, and continued to fight for my kids for a better life."

Throughout her journey, she turned adversities into opportunities. Having a strong desire to be present for her kids allowed her to have the strength she needs to keep going.

"No matter what you're going through, there's a light at the end of the tunnel, and it may seem hard to get to, but you can do it and just keep working towards it and you'll find the positive side in things."
- Demi Lovato

What is your deepest desire in life?
Do you know what is it?

If you can't find your heart's desire, find something that scares you the most.

What's your biggest fear?

To me, it was continuing to live in a dysfunctional family. Extreme conflict everywhere, fighting and yelling at each other, followed by physical or emotional abuse. It was a cycle being carried within the family from my grandfather to my father, and now to us.

As a result, we also didn't have enough money to cover the necessities in life. I wore a mask each time I stepped out, pretending I had it all together, that everything was perfect. I lived in survival mode each day of my life, longing for peace, love, happiness, comfort, freedom not only for myself but also for my family.

I was scared to lose all respect for my father, knowing that he was also a victim himself of the trauma carried across generations in our family. I knew that if I didn't take action, I would stay where I was. Most of all, I was heartbroken every time I saw the people I cared for, my mom, my siblings, even my dad, consumed by the toxic environment and suffering as a victim of the situation.

I realized I had many fears at the time. But I came to understand that the pain of staying where I had been, was greater than the pain of changing to pursue my desire. This fueled my desire to take action.

Only by taking one step at a time, my life changed. Each step led me down the path towards my ultimate destination. It opened the door to the next opportunity and connected me to the right people. It helped me find the resources needed to make things happen.

Over to you:

Allow yourself to be open and think without any limitations when answering the following questions.

1. If resources like time, money, people, the place were not an issue, what would I do?

    You may have identified your dream in the previous chapter. In this section, you will assess if you have the desire to pursue the dream you identified. If not, you can reflect upon and assess which dream gave you unyielding desire.

2. If my life had absolutely no limits, what would I choose to have and what would I choose to do?

3. What's standing in the way of achieving it?

4. What will happen if I don't take this step?

5. If my main obstacle didn't exist, how would my life look?

CHAPTER 3
MAKE DECISIONS AND TAKE ACTION

Growth means change, and change involves risk, stepping from the known to the unknown.
– George Shinn

I was twenty-three years old, single, and lived with my parents. I worked in a manufacturing company as an IT software engineer. I got a high-paying job with excellent benefits. Things were going well in my career.

After a few years, the excitement I used to have when I started the job changed to boredom. I felt complacent. I had this tug of war between my fear and my inner voice. The little voice inside of me was constantly reminding me to explore.

If you are not happy where you're at, explore the options to make it better. If you tried different possibilities and nothing changed, it's a good sign it's time to make your next move. Leave the situation, change it, or accept it.

I recognized that I wanted a change, not only in my career but also in another aspect of my life. I was longing for something. I wanted to move to another place and to bring my mom with me, away from my dad, away from all the drama in life. Although money wasn't the most important thing for me, it played a significant role in making things happen.

I had a few friends, who'd been living and working in Singapore for years, who shared their stories with me. I realized, working abroad would pay me three times or more, compared to what I could make in the Philippines, especially if your expertise is in IT. I was encouraged by their lifestyle and experiences. More than that, the idea of being away from the toxic situation at home, opportunities to grow and earn more was incredibly appealing. So, I made my decision, planned, and prepared for my journey.

I saved enough money to cover my expenses for six months. I reached out to my networks, researched about lifestyle and cultural adjustment in Singapore, and applied for jobs online. Then I gave my two weeks notice. I quit my job and started my adventure.

When I handed in my resignation, I received a counteroffer. My employer offered better benefits, a salary increase, department change, name it, and they would negotiate. I felt like a more valuable employee, but I had made up my mind. I knew no matter what happened; I was up for a change.

The moment you accept the responsibility to take control of your life, the harder it is to resist the temptation to stay in your comfort zone.

Why leave if it is comfortable?
Are you afraid of stepping into the unknown?

Have the courage to say NO. Pursue what matters to you most. Take the risk. Make the change in life that is worth making

You may be stepping into the unknown, but what's the worst thing that can happen?

You fail, learn, and grow. Try once more. If you fail again, at least fail better. And the next time, you'll do well until you get what you want.

Failure is the steppingstone to success if you learn from it. It became part of your past and served as an experience that shaped your character.

As what Neale Donald Walsch quoted, "Life begins at the end of your comfort zone."

Would you rather live a life pursuing what you wanted or live a life full of what-ifs and regret?

The decision is yours. **When you decide, stand by it.** Remember, for us to grow, choose courage over comfort because we can't have both.

"I want to be in the arena. I want to be brave in my life. And when we make the choice to dare greatly, we sign up to get our asses kicked. We can choose courage, or we can choose comfort, but we can't have both."
– Brené Brown

Thoughts to ponder:

It is so easy to get caught up in the analysis-paralysis state. It occurs when you overthink and underperform — considering all the possible outcomes before deciding. The cold truth is, you can't be 100% sure of everything.

Life is short, and nothing is guaranteed. The decisions you make today have a significant impact on the life you live.

If you are not where you wanted to be, ask yourself, what can I do today to be where I want to be?

MANAGING DECISIONS

Making a decision is the first step, but it doesn't mean it will make things better. Every day, I have to remind myself, "Is what I do supporting the fulfillment of my goal based on the decision I made?"

Good decision-making is an essential life skill, but most of the time, it takes a while and some practice to get good at it. Here are some common negative scripts which come up in our minds when we need to decide. Allow yourself to become aware of them, so they do not affect or stop you from making that decision:

- I'm no longer effective.
- I'm not growing anymore.
- I'm stuck.
- I'm just doing this for the sake of….
- I get very anxious about this.
- I'm a victim.
- I have no way out.

- I'm too old (or too young)
- I'm broke.
- I'm lost.

Or when I feel…
- I wanted out.
- I'm sick of the situation or probably want CHANGE.

How you choose to label yourself becomes who you are. When you label yourself based on your limitations, you limit your potential to grow. Instead of doing, you unconsciously allow yourself to dwell upon the past situations. You're programming your mind with limiting beliefs by repeating these scripts every day.

It is important to recognize the limiting belief you have to take the first step. Most limiting beliefs are subconscious, so it may take some work to uncover them. Here are some questions you can ask yourself to identify your own self-limiting beliefs:

- What action should I take to support my deepest desire?
- What can I do now to support my decision?
- If I don't do this now, will I regret it?
- What's the best thing that can happen if I follow-through?
- What're the worst things can happen?
- How am I committed to this change?
- What is the belief behind my limiting belief?

Understanding your self-limiting beliefs may take some time.

Remember to align your words and your thoughts on the outcome you want. Decide to overcome the limiting belief you have.

<hr />

I excelled in school and at work, but I was wearing a mask. When I wanted to make the change at work, I realized it was because of unresolved issues I had in my personal life.

I refused to talk to my dad for years. I was terrified that he could hurt me when he was drunk. I spent most of my life in my room. It was small, with a single bed attached to the wall, drawer, and bedside lamp. It was my quiet place. I only stepped out when I went for a shower or needed to leave the house. Every day, my mom knocked at my door to pass me a plate with rice and food.

In one corner of my room, I spent time seeking answers to how things could get better. One night, I read a free subscription book I received from Joyce Meyer. It talked about finding direction and peace in life. It said that sometimes, you need to be in a different place, to find the peace you are searching. Followed by a verse quoted from the Bible, *"Seek you first the Kingdom of God and all his righteousness will be added unto you"* – *Matthew 6:33*

It struck me! I kept it in my heart and it became my life verse. It was another confirmation for me to follow through with my decision. I had the desire to earn more money, find a place for myself and my mom to move and to have a better life. But this time, I had clarity and confidence; if I found the peace I was longing for first, through HIM, the rest would follow.

Roy T. Bennett said, "Your beliefs affect your choices. Your choices shape your actions. Your actions determine your results. The future you create depends upon the choices you make and the actions you take today."

⁓⁓

Before working at my last job in the Philippines, I had a contract to go to Taiwan. It was an operator job in a semiconductor manufacturing company.

You might be wondering, why did I accept that role if I have a Computer Science degree?

First, the salary was three times higher than the average income for IT professionals in the Philippines. Second, the idea of living abroad is exciting for a young adult who's never been away from her homeland. A new place, away from everybody I knew, a place where I could start all over again.

Successful candidates required a placement fee before onboarding. It was the amount to pay for the recruitment agency as compensation for hiring me for an overseas job. It would cover the flight as well. I was 22 years old and didn't have enough savings. I needed my parents' help to make it happen.

I discussed the opportunity with my mom, and she passed it

along to my dad. They were supportive, so I applied for it. My parents assured me that they would cover the fee. They encouraged me throughout the application to do what's needed. I completed my medical exams and all other requirements, except for the placement fee. Little did I know, they didn't have that large sum of money. They planned to use our house as collateral for a loan to cover it.

One morning, my father said, "It's not a good move to use our equity for this."

I looked at him and felt devastated.

"You should have told me earlier, so I didn't spend all this time and energy to work on all these requirements." I exploded. "I would understand if you told me earlier, but instead, you gave me false hope," I screamed and walked away.

I was heartbroken. I promised myself not to depend on anyone else next time I plan to go or work abroad. I would earn every penny I needed to support myself to make things happen.

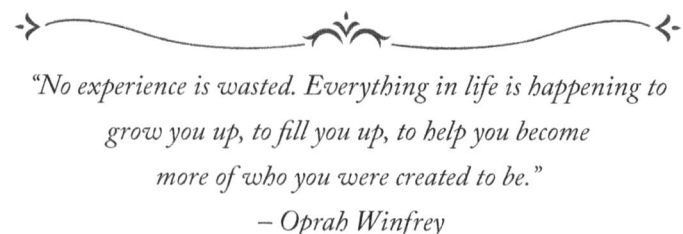

"No experience is wasted. Everything in life is happening to grow you up, to fill you up, to help you become more of who you were created to be."
– Oprah Winfrey

When you make a decision, you'll be surprised how the universe will lead you to the right people and resources to make it happen. This is what happened to me when I decided to explore the opportunities in Singapore.

My cousin Tina and her family visited us. They had lived in Singapore for more than a decade.

"Stay with us if you go to Singapore, we'll have a room ready for you," she said.

Excited to hear what she offered, I worked on my timeline and prepared for my next venture. As it turned out, that decision to take a leap of faith was the best decision I had made in my career up to that point.

Stepping into the Unknown

As the plane took off, I felt so lost. I didn't know where I was going, but it felt like someone held my hand, whispering: *"It's going to be alright, I'm with you, I got your back."*

I trusted the voice and pondered on the verse that struck me through the entire trip. *"Seek you first the kingdom of God and all his righteousness will be added unto you."* -Matthew 6:33

At that time, I wasn't clear about what it meant, but one thing I know for sure, it gave me peace and comfort in my heart.

Change broadens your experiences, perspective, and can help you grow.

Keep an Open Mind

I arrived safely and was excited to begin my journey. As I walked through the gate, I spotted my cousin, Tinah, with her family.

"Welcome Marge!" she exclaimed then hugged me. She introduced her four kids, who were a couple of years younger than me. "We're going to Sunday service first since it's pretty close here!"

Clueless what Sunday service was, I smiled and said: "Totally up for it."

Guess where my first destination was?

Live band. Loud music. Uplifting, cheerful melodies. Gleaming lights. Large crowd. Stylish people were singing and dancing. I thought I was at a concert, but what a big surprise. I was in the Church! It was a different ambiance.

Suddenly, the music stopped. A man in a nice black suit gave an hour-long talk about faith and life circumstances. It was quite a surprising experience for me, but I kept an open mind.

Tinah said it would be a good place for me to start. It could help me to connect with others, since I was looking for a job and get encouraged with the message as well.

Since the airport was near to the church, I didn't mind at all. Also, I had no clue where I was, so I trusted her recommendation. After the service, I met a few Indonesians and fellow Filipinos on the same path. Like me, they were taking their chance in a foreign land, searching for jobs in a different field for different reasons.

Tinah introduced me to one of the leaders in a youth group, GJ, a fellow Filipino, who had lived and worked in Singapore for more than a decade. We spoke for a bit, then she introduced me to some of her friends. Later, I noticed I was already part of a big crowd. Connecting and socializing with a bunch of young people of different races. Most of them had colorful outfits, fancy hair color, and stylish hairstyles.

I felt overwhelmed on my first day in a foreign land. The first time in my life to ride a plane. The first time to be separated from my family. First time to surround myself with different races and speak in English all the time. The first time to step into the unknown.

It's not that I've always known I would have a better future when I stepped out of my comfort zone. It was very clear to me that if I stayed where I was, I would be destroyed. I knew I couldn't let that happen. I recognized I was the only one left who could end the trauma in my family.

I was overwhelmed but enjoyed the process as I kept my eyes open to possibilities. I was confident it would lead to something bigger. Keeping an open mind allowed me to see life from a different perspective. It allowed me to see things I could never imagine.

Start with Why

As I achieved some of my dreams and desires, I met people who were traveling on the same path but had just started on their journey. One of my close friends, Jen, introduced me to Lut and Ivy. They are fellow students from my university, also majored in Computer Science and worked in the same company as me before coming to Singapore.

When connecting with people in the group, I asked questions to find their purpose: Why did you come here? Why did you leave your homeland? Why choose to work here and not in other places? Where do you want to go a year from now once you get the job? How about five years from now?

It is not common for someone to leave his or her homeland, move to another country to look for a job, and get an offer in a week or two. Having clarity about the purpose would determine how far you could go to achieve your goals.

In Start with Why: How Great Leaders Inspire Everyone to Take Action, Simon Sinek wrote, "We want to be around people and organizations who are like us and share our beliefs."

Starting with WHY allows like-minded people to identify with you on a personal level. If your WHY matches their WHY, they are willing to stand with you through thick and thin. Without a clear WHY, people default to the WHAT. Then you are always caught in this struggle to separate yourself from WHAT.

Lut and Ivy both smiled and were surprised as they thought about how to respond. After they gained clarity on their WHYs, they felt more prepared for their journey. It was not only looking for a job. There was a deeper reason behind it; they wanted to advance their career and provide a better life for their family. Knowing that we had the same whys, I offered the support needed together with other mentors who guided me.

The group continued to increase. In less than a year, we formed a young professional group. Members who used to be like me, people looking for a better opportunity, then eventually found jobs. We came from different fields in IT, Engineering, Architect, Dentistry, Sales, Hotel Industry and many more. We were a bunch of young people welcoming others and supporting one another. We saw how each other grew in their faith as they traveled through their journey in Singapore.

Over to you:

In the previous chapter, you have identified your deepest desire. Now it's time to take the necessary actions to make it happen. It's time to take a step towards making that decision.

Here are some questions you can reflect on to help you identify that big decision:

1. What action should I take to support my deepest desire?
2. What are my priorities now in my life?
3. With the priorities I have now, what can I do to support my decision?
4. If I can't jump to make a big change yet, what is the smallest thing I can I do now to get started?
5. If I don't do this now, will I regret it?
6. What's the best thing that can happen if I follow through?
7. What are the worst things can happen?
8. Is this decision aligned with my values?
9. What's my timeline?
10. How committed am I to this change?

Once you have pondered on the questions above, I recommend you write a contract for yourself. It will serve as an instrument to reprogram your subconscious mind if you reflect on it daily.

COMMITMENT TO MAKE THINGS HAPPEN

Take a look at the statement below. Reflect on what it will mean to you, then fill it out and sign it.

I, _____, commit myself today to
_____
_____
_____
_____
_____

_____

_____

_____

I recognize that no matter what my circumstances are, I will take one step at a time. I will continue to progress in my journey. I will do what it takes to make this happen.

Signature: _____ Date: _____

Once you fill this out, sign, print it and post it in a place that will remind you every single day of your decision.

Remember: What you focus on expands!

CHAPTER 4
THE PEOPLE YOU MEET ALONG THE WAY

Some people come into our lives and quickly go. Some people move our souls to dance. They awaken us to a new understanding with a passing whisper of their wisdom. Some people make the sky more beautiful to gaze upon. They stay in our lives for a while, leave footprints in our hearts, and we are never ever the same.
– author unknown

We meet people for a reason. Every single one we meet has a role in our lives, be it big or small. It could be a lesson in our lives, a helping hand to figure out who you are and who you want to become. Either you need them to change your life, or you're the one who will change theirs.

Ever since I started my journey to step into the unknown, I have been more than grateful for the people who have come into my life. I've experienced the importance of random people that showed up in my life that turned out to be the reason for me to rise up. Here's my story on how I decided to help others, because of the people who crossed my path and had sown into my life.

I went to Sunday service for the first few weekends for different reasons. The first one, I did it as a favor for my cousin. Eventually, I continued to come on my own to network with people and understand the culture. But there were times I didn't like to join them. I wanted to be alone and questioned my decision. I missed my mom, the paycheque, company benefits, or better to say, my comfort zone.

During those times, I went to the mall, park, library, or any other place. I could escape instead of joining them. In those times, I felt sad, unsure of what the future would bring, doubting my decision to step into the unknown. Then, one of these times I got an unexpected call.

"Hey Marge, this is GJ, how are you?" she asked.
"I'm good; what's up?" I responded.
"How's the job-hunting progressing? Is there any way I can help?" she said.

That's how we always started our conversation, and then we talked about life and family. It ended most of the time when she asked me if I could meet with her for lunch or dinner.

Although I answered her calls and enjoyed the conversations, I refused to meet her. I had that feeling she would ask me to join their prayer group or other activities. But no matter how many times I turned her down, she kept reaching out. She gave her best effort to continue to connect with me. Finally, one day, I started to feel down and I thought I could get some support to keep going. So, I finally decided to meet up with her.

She asked me to meet up with her in her office. Despite her busy schedule, she squeezed me in for lunch. During the one-hour meeting we had, I felt I had a purposeful conversation. She listened and shared her story. She gave me many tools I needed to be more effective in job hunting. Most of all, she encouraged me, walked with me, and prayed together with me on my journey. Definitely not what I was expecting.

GJ didn't bring up anything related to the church, faith, or any activities. I had thought she would ask me to go there. I realized she had no other intention for me, but good. I felt the joy to experience it from someone I just met, and not even from someone related to me. Unconditional love which I rarely saw before.

That was the start of my friendship with GJ. Because of what she had sown into my life, I learned to do the same thing to others. She continued to encourage me and mentors me even now.

Later on, I decided to join other activities where she was involved. It led me to become an active member of the youth cell group. We talked more about hobbies, arts, skills, and life in general. We had different events to support young professionals looking for better job opportunities and study groups for young people in school. Every Friday, I was looking forward to hanging out with the new people I met, praying with them. I felt loved and supported.

The favor I did for my cousin when I first came to the church ended up becoming a favor for me. I met fun, caring, and loving people who made my adjustment to a foreign land easier. I learned to step out of my comfort zone again and again. Each move I made, I felt supported and encouraged by the people with the same values and interests as mine. What Theodore Roosevelt said, *"People don't care how much you know until they know how much you care"* was a true testimony for me. It became my mantra for life.

It is important to remember when you're making a shift to identifying your support group. If you don't have one yet, keep asking and praying/meditating for it.

You will be surprised how this will be revealed to you if you trust the process.

Rania Naim of Thought Catalog writes on her blog: "Sometimes the stage of your life determines what kind of people you attract and I think that's the beauty of faith, God sends you the people you need at exactly the right time. He gives you the answers you were looking for through these people. He enlightens you by bringing you closer to people who bring out the best in you. He helps you when you're struggling by pulling you closer to those who are capable of digging you out of your darkness.

It's just that sometimes we try to turn these temporary people into forever people, but that's not their role. They're not meant to stay in our lives forever. God called them to be there for us for only a short period. God called them to be in our lives so they can make us better for the ones who are meant to stay forever."

Over to you:

Everything that happens around us, as a result of the people in our lives, is what needs to occur. Someone had rightly said, 'We don't meet people by accident. They are meant to cross our path for a reason.

1. Think of three people you've met in your life that brighten your day when you are feeling down.

2. Now, think of one person not related to you that could offer some support, help, or simple encouragement. What is the one simple thing you can do to touch someone's life?

Go and make someone smile!

CHAPTER 5
DELAY IS NOT DENIAL

God's Delays Are Not God's denials.
- Robert H. Schuller

Great dreams do not come to pass greatly at a twinkle of an eye, but you may see them happening at a twinkle of an eye. The best dream which survives greatly in reality, takes great roots first before it grows in reality to bear great fruits. Delay is not death! Carefully and patiently nurture your dreams and make them happen distinctively in reality.
- Ernest Agyemang Yeboah

Have you worked on a goal that has yet to be fulfilled? Have you felt you've given it all but are still waiting? Are you still not getting the results you want?

Waiting is perhaps one of life's most difficult tasks. When the going gets tough, it is hard to stay positive and stay on track. It is easier to look at it as a denial of what you want instead of recognizing it as another "delay" in life. But the fact of life is, delays are an everyday occurrence. Delays always occur at some point in our lives.

This is the same thing I encountered when I looked for a better job opportunity in Singapore. I was in a place away from my father, surrounded by new friends that cared for and supported me. I felt inspired and enjoyed my journey. I knew it was only a matter of timing to get a job offer, but my savings were running out. My limited time was coming to an end and I didn't get a job offer yet.

As a tourist in Singapore, my time was limited to the length of my visitor's pass. An extension can usually be granted for up to three months, but how long you get is up to the officer's discretion.

On my first entry, I was given two weeks. I didn't get a job offer at that time. I went to all the job fairs and applied in every way I could.

Determined to get an offer, I extended as much as I could. Every single day, I gave my best to reach my goal. I used all of my networks. I prayed and believed that my journey would end well. I felt I had given it my all, but sometimes, despite all the hard work and sacrifices we put in, we don't always get what we want.

My goal to get a job fast didn't happen as I planned. I had many interviews, but when they heard that I wasn't a resident or citizen, the chance to get a second interview disappeared. As the time got closer to my visitor's pass expiration, I felt nervous. It meant I would have to ask for another extension with no assurance I would get it.

When rejection hits you, the best place to go is to revisit your Whys. The "Why" that defines your Dream, Desire and Decision.

Why did I come here in the first place?
Why did I quit my high-paying job?
Why did I leave my family?

One day, Edmund, one of GJ's mentors from the youth group, asked me about my long-term plans. I shared stories about my search for better opportunities and the struggles I encountered on the way. I had a limited time in Singapore and still no offers. But I had a backup plan, to return to my previous employer if I didn't succeed.

Edmund shared words of wisdom about not being double-minded and trusting myself alone in the process. He encouraged me to know what my deepest desire was and to stay laser focused. To learn not just to trust myself but trust God in my life.

I realized my backup plan didn't exist before. It only came out as a result of not achieving my goal based on my timeline. I made myself believe there were options, so, if I didn't succeed, it wouldn't be so bad.

I worked hard to pursue my goal, but in times of difficulty, the faith I believe I had vanished. I looked at my "Delays" as a sign to go back to my old ways and comfortable situations.

I realized that if I truly wanted to progress in life, I had to experience the entire process, not just part of it. My delay wasn't denial. It was a result of the decisions I made that lead to pain and rejection. An experience I had to embrace as part of my growth journey to achieve my goal. The pain when a delay happens is an opportunity to increase faith in what one believes in. In God and myself that everything will turn out for the best in the end.

After that moment, I felt enlightened. I had a sudden change in my mindset. My "why" transformed into something bigger when I gained clarity. I knew I needed a lifestyle change that would last. I could only do it in a place where I could empower myself, apart from all the pains I experienced. I had a desire to grow not only in my career but also in other aspects of my life.

Determined to make the change for good, it tested my faith. Every day, I woke up early in the morning and confessed, "Something great is going to happen today. I will get an offer but according to HIS plan and not mine." I reminded myself of the verse I was holding on to: *"But seek first the kingdom of God and his righteousness, and all these things will be added to you."*

One time, I walked to City Hall all by myself. I noticed my shoes getting worn out because of those days walking all day to get a job. Then I looked up in the sky and whispered, *"I am running out of time, but I am trusting you. I know you have plans for me."*

⁓⁂⁓

I went to immigration for another extension. As I lined up, a man talked to me in a different language.

"I'm sorry. I don't understand," I asked puzzledly.
He replied, "You're Indonesian, right?"
I responded, "No, I'm not."

He smiled at me and said, "God is good. He has plans for you. It's now your turn," while pointing to the immigration officer.

And he was right; it was my turn to talk to the officer. I asked for another extension, but it was denied. I explained to him that my two-year long-term employment pass application was in progress.

"No more extension, you need to go back." The officer said.
I replied, "I have my employment pass. It's being processed."
"Come back when it's processed then!" the officer exclaimed.

Employment Pass Eligibility Certificate (EPEC) issued foreign professionals a 6-12 months visa to stay in the country and pursue job-hunting. Although the program was discontinued in 2011, at that time in 2006, I had the approval for my application. The problem was that I had to wait for the certificate to be mailed to me to prove to the officers. An online reference number wasn't enough at that time.

After two months of job hunting in Singapore, I had to leave. I turned around and whispered to myself, "All things work together for good." I looked around. I didn't see the Indonesian man who talked to me. He wasn't there anymore.

Ambivalent. I sat down under the tree while I waited for the bus. Thinking not only of my dreams but of my family. My desire to have a better life. I felt broken, but instead of dwelling on my emotions, I pulled out my bible.

As I opened it, the verse that popped up, "Trust in the LORD with all your heart and lean not on your own understanding; in all thy ways acknowledge him, and he shall direct thy paths."
- Proverbs 3:5-6

With tears in my eyes, I looked up in the sky, and exclaimed, "I'm leaving this into your hands." I didn't get the job I was looking for, but I had found peace.

What you don't understand now, things that you're going through, if you just keep going, and have faith in God and fully surrender to him, he will give you peace in your heart.

It doesn't make sense to you or anybody but you know in your heart it's worth it and at the right time…later on, you will look back and say, "Now, I understand….It made me a better person"

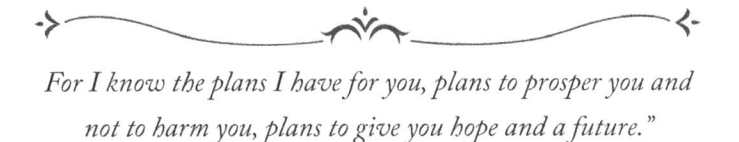

For I know the plans I have for you, plans to prosper you and not to harm you, plans to give you hope and a future."
- Jeremiah 29:11

Over to you:

In the previous chapters, you have identified your desire and taken action. Now, it's time to revisit where you stand after taking these actions.

1. Think of a "Delay" in your life that you're currently facing or recently encountered.

2. Now, how did you handle it, or how will you handle it?

    If you are not 100% convinced that you have done your best, what's stopping you from trying again? What was your "Why" when you pursued it on the first place?

Delayed doesn't mean Denied. If you encounter delays, I encourage you to focus on things you can control. Sometimes, the best thing you could do is to keep your head up and keep going. Embrace the situation, allow yourself to experience the pain of unmet expectations, but don't give up on your dream.

Here are some affirmations, a prayer/ meditation you can use when you are dealing with "Delays" in your life. Take a moment to reflect with an open heart and mind.

- I will commit to reminding myself of all the times it has all worked out in my favor in the end.
- If it hasn't worked out yet, it's not the end.
- I trust the process.
- I embrace the journey
- I will not let disappointment prevent me from pushing forward with a positive mindset and outlook.

Prayer for Serenity

God, grant me the serenity

to accept the things I cannot change,

the courage to change the things I can,

and the wisdom to know the difference.

Living one day at a time,

enjoying one moment at a time;

accepting hardship as a pathway to peace;

taking, as Jesus did,

this sinful world as it is,

not as I would have it;

trusting that You will make all things right

if I surrender to Your will;

so that I may be reasonable happy in this life

and supremely happy with You forever in the next.

Amen.

- Reinhold Niebuhr

CHAPTER 6
LET GO AND LET GOD

Let go and let God. Let Him take over your life and run it. He knows how.
— *Norman Vincent Peale*

When you have done everything you need to do, the things you can't control, you have to let go and let God, and when you give it to him, you have to give it ALL.

God's delay is not denial.

I decided to leave it up to God and headed to my last interview. After my interview, I told my friends and relatives that my request for an extension was denied. I returned to my room and cried it all out to him. I bawled, "God, I'm scared. I have this fire burning; I'm growing, I'm free here. I'm scared to lose all these things, the joy and peace you placed in my heart when I go home. I want to help my mom; I want to help my siblings. I want to do more for your glory, but I will do what you want me to do."

With or without God, good decisions can be made; But only with God will great decisions be made.
- Damon Thueson

After I poured out my heart and all my tears had fallen, I accepted the situation and submitted everything to Him. I trusted Him to guide me through whatever happened next in my life. I flew back home to the Philippines with peace in my heart and faith in him. But faith without action is death, so I worked on my plan to improve myself. I planned to come back to Singapore again, but during the waiting period, I would get all my certifications and a temporary job that would pay well for six months.

After everything I had experienced when I stepped into the unknown, I was clear that I wanted to live in Singapore. I wanted to be in a place where I had an active community that would allow me to grow as an Individual and earn significantly more than what I used to get in my previous job.

I had proven that during my stay there. I thought I was just looking for a job, but it was more than that, there was a bigger purpose. I was looking to get to know more about myself and more about life.

Staying focused on my plans and trusting that HE is with me.

Having a plan in place allowed me to have a roadmap for what to do next. I continued to apply for jobs in Singapore. I enrolled in different courses to improve my skills while waiting for a job offer. I knew I needed to become more competitive in the marketplace. I would bring my transcripts and other required certifications the next time I went back to Singapore.

"When you are in troubled and worried and sick at heart, And your plans are upset, and your world falls apart, Remember God's ready and waiting to share The burden you find much to heavy to bear-- So with faith, "Let Go and Let GOD" lead your way Into a brighter and less troubled day." - Helen Steiner Rice

Over to you:

Have you decided to go-on with something, even when everything you got turned out in a way you didn't expect? Use the following questions to guide you in your journey:

1. What lessons have you learned?
2. Are you grateful for this experience?
3. How can you turn the situation into success?
4. Who else has failed in this way before, and how can you learn from his/her experience?

Give yourself some time when things aren't going your way. Continue to hold on to His promises. If you have done everything you can, what else you could do but to leave it to God.

Give all your worries and cares to God,
for he cares about you.
- 1 Peter 5:7

Come to me, all who labor and are heavy laden,
and I will give you rest.
- Matthew 11:28

CHAPTER 7
FORGIVENESS

Holding on to anger, resentment and hurt only gives you tense muscles, a headache and a sore jaw from clenching your teeth. Forgiveness gives you back the laughter and the lightness in your life.
- Joan Lunden

Is there someone you haven't forgiven? Someone who said "I'm sorry" but you doubt their sincerity? Are you ready to forgive?

Forgiveness is easier said than done. It's hard to forgive people, especially if we were greatly offended by someone we love.

This is the situation I've encountered when my father asked for forgiveness for the very first time. I refused to forgive him. I wasn't ready. I just couldn't, or should I say wasn't willing at that time.

Growing up, I felt terrified to see my mom in pain and beaten up. In those days, I stood up for her; my father turned his rage against me. I'd scream and cry as he would beat me.

I yelled, "I didn't do anything; it wasn't me. Stop, please stop. Don't hurt my mom. I'll shut up, just please don't hurt her, please."

I'd limp to my room sobbing hysterically and just wanted to vanish. I wanted to grow up fast, get a job, and have my own money so I could get us out. I walked on eggshells every day.

Coming home from school or work was terrifying. When my father got home, I would wonder, is he drunk? Is he coming downstairs to my room? Is my mom okay? Are we safe tonight? When I heard him around, my heart would pound out of my chest. I'd curl up on my bed and brace myself.

It was constant. I battled surviving in a toxic situation inside my home since I was in elementary school. I felt powerless being young. All I wanted at that time was to grow up so I could get out.

When he got drunk, he stormed into my room and yelled at me.

"Leave! this is my house, my place".
"You're not going to be successful at all."
"You're no good. You'll be a commodity for men."
"You're a bad influence on your mom! You just wanted us to separate!"
"You…You…You…"

These are his words that struck me for years. I struggled with pain, anger, and frustration with the labels my father gave me.

Physical pain heals, but the abusive words got stuck in my head for years. Emotional abuse is so silent and elusive that I could put up with it for years, without even knowing. If it's not settled, it becomes a trauma that could be passed across generations.

As I got older, I learned to fight back. When my father told me again to leave the house, I responded. *"This is not just yours, but mama's too. I have my rights. You should leave, not me!"*

Of course, it made his blood boil with rage. He raised his hand to slap me, but my mom grabbed it first. I sprinted to my room, locked my door, and stayed there till he left. The great thing was, the first time that I stood up for myself; I felt empowered to speak up more.

We were living in the same house, but since I stood up for myself, he avoided me when he was sober. Growing up, I couldn't stand to look or speak to him. He made it clear that if someone had to leave, it should be me. I wanted to move out but didn't have enough savings.

I remember coming home from school or work and would go directly to my room, turning the doorknob filled with crippling fear. My mom would pass the food to me every meal. She knew the tension between my father and me and kept me away from him.

She convinced my father to go to another place when I needed to step out or use the washroom. Although it worked most of the time, there were times we bumped into each other. We either ignored each other or provoked one another if our paths crossed.

I applaud my mom for being a martyr. Despite all the physical and emotional abuse from my father, she stayed with him and didn't abandon us. She could have left us a long time ago, but she sacrificed. Although she's been my inspiration, it gave me clarity at my young age about what I wanted in life. I wouldn't be a martyr for someone who hurt the people I love.

When you've been battling for your survival for a long time, it forces you to toughen up.

I focused on my purpose. Set my mind on things I could control and forgot the ones I couldn't.

No matter how big the issues were in my family, I left them behind as I stepped out of the house. I learned to be more resilient. Living in a dysfunctional family was a constant struggle to deal with. I lived in survival mode, but it pushed me to give my best in other areas of life.

My pay continued to increase at work. My savings continued to grow. I served in the youth group in the church. I plugged into the youth ministry, shared my skills in dancing and creativity. I joined extracurricular activities at school. Painting, dancing, and other things that kept me occupied.

I worked on my side-hustles. I offered computer repairs without renting space in my father's house. I provided services such as hardware or software upgrades, and installations. I taught computer courses to college students part-time. I also provided basic computer courses to baby boomers.

I didn't have the energy to dwell on more drama in life. I kept myself occupied and did my best to excel in other areas.

While climbing the ladder to reach my goals kept me busy, the situation with my family remained. Later, I realized my brothers had grown and dealt with the same battles in their lives.

One night, one of my brothers went to the bar with his friends to perform in a band. Surprised, he saw my father with other women. Shamed with the situation, he walked away and told his friends to ignore it. He shared his pain with my mom. My brother felt hurt, embarrassed, mad, and disappointed with my father.

My mom wanted a divorce. But even on those occasions, when my father got caught cheating, he twisted the situation and made her feel bad. But at that time, he couldn't lie to us anymore.

He begged and promised, told her that he would change for the good. My mom knew how much her kids struggled with him around, and myself, the only daughter, suffered most. She asked him to ask for forgiveness from us. So, he did.

Forgiving is hard, but not forgiving hurts

At that time, I felt I was on a roller coaster of numbness and pain — a chaotic situation. The pain turned into bitterness. There was no more trust left. How can you forgive someone who hurt you and the people you love? And the worst part of all, he said sorry but kept doing the same thing over and over.

"You never stop hurting us! You lied and kept doing the same thing over and over! No, I can't forgive you," I raged.

I guess I had reached my limit. I wanted to forgive because it's the right thing to do but I couldn't. I wasn't ready. It wasn't only the last thing he did; it was all that pain buried in my heart for years. And possibly more things he would do in the future.

Denying forgiveness to my father didn't make the situation any better. For a moment, I felt good, but the long-term effects were not.

I excelled at work and at school. I impressed the people around me for being an achiever and for being focused. But It was all just a mask. I'd wear my mask to show that everything was going well.

No matter how good it looked outside, I was suffering and depressed inside. Hatred, resentment, anger, bitterness had all grown in my heart. I couldn't get past what life had thrown at me. I was only going through the motions. No matter how hard I tried, I wasn't moving forward.

My mom respected my decision, but it made my relationship with my dad worse. He kicked me out of the house. He felt threatened that my presence would ruin his marriage. Every time he attacked her, I sprinted in front of my mom and shouted at him to stop, then he turned to me.

This was my life for almost a decade. I'd been in the same battle with my father for so long that the pain turned to numbness. I couldn't stop him from hurting us, so I focused on what I could do. I had to survive to find a way out so I could help the rest of my family too.

When I decided to go to Singapore, it wasn't only for a better job opportunity; it was because I wanted to get out of the chaotic world of a dysfunctional family. It would be a bonus to get a job that paid well and fulfill the rest of my goals.

On the day of my first flight to Singapore, at the airport, my mom wept as she waved goodbye to me. It was hard letting her only daughter go, but she knew it would be for the better. She let go of me and trusted my future in God's hands, especially in those times she wouldn't be around.

A Story of Forgiveness

During one of the Sunday services in Singapore, the Pastor preached about forgiveness. At the end of the service, he asked the audience to stand up.

With soft music playing in the background, he said, *"Put your hands together. Think of the person or the people that hurt you. Think about how they influenced your life. Take your time and remember how they impacted you. You have them in your hands."*

I thought of my father. I felt stabbed many times by all the pain I had experienced. I felt my family suffered because of him. I thought of my mom's pain for staying with him, my siblings. I had an endless list of people that caused me pain, including myself. It was too hard on myself. It was a flashback of traumatic experiences in my life.

And then the Pastor said, "You suffered and are still suffering. You got stuck. You struggled for years. It wasn't easy, even up to now, you're still hurting. Think of God's love, Think of your father's unconditional love. And say, I forgive you while opening your hands and release to God."

It took a long time for me to do it. But with God's help, I did it. I released it to him. I took the first step. I decided to forgive.

What happened next surprised me. I wept like a hungry baby longing for her mom's milk. I longed for my father's love. I had a hard time growing up, looking for a father figure for years. I was in deep pain.

At that moment, I felt a light sparked inside me. Even though my biological father had hurt me, my father in heaven loved the way I am and never left me. In those times I couldn't walk, he carried me. When I was in the wilderness, he comforted me, and he helped me to focus on what I could do to take one step at a time. He loved me more than anyone else could.

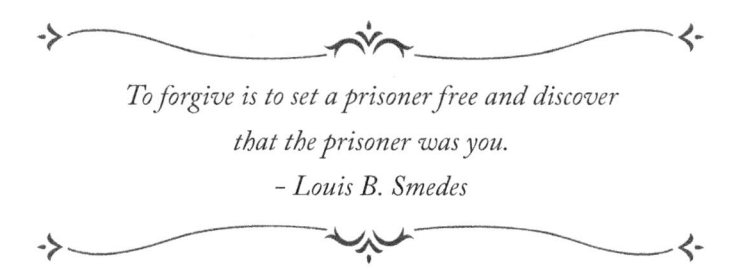

To forgive is to set a prisoner free and discover that the prisoner was you.
- Louis B. Smedes

Forgiveness is a Decision

This story is about my experience when I first faced the person that had deeply hurt me, my father, and how I decided to forgive.

On my first day, when I arrived back from Singapore, I sat at the table with my family.

I looked at my father and asked, "How was the traffic today when you went to the market?"

He cocked an eyebrow in surprise and responded, "…not so bad."

My youngest brother eyes popped wide as he heard the conversation happening between my father and me. He knew it'd been years since I last talked to him, what happened also amazed me!

That night, in the same tiny little room where I had spent most of my childhood and poured out my tears, I reflected upon my life and examined my heart. I didn't feel the anger and hatred anymore. I had forgiven my father. I felt peace.

I opened the bible and the first verse that showed up: "Do unto others what you want others to do unto you…"

I wept as He spoke into my heart. Forgiveness, Love, Courage, Resilience, Determination, how could I share his words to others without experiencing it myself? I found the clarity about the questions I had about my journey.

No more hatred. I let go. I had forgiven my father; I had forgiven myself.

Forgiveness doesn't mean forgetting. The person who caused your pain might not deserve your forgiveness, but you deserve to be at peace. When you forgive someone, it doesn't mean that you condone their behavior or tolerate any further abuse or lack of respect. **When you forgive, you set yourself free.**

How many times have you heard, "You must forgive." or "You need to forgive and forget."?

Perhaps a hundred times or more. The thing is, forgiving may be easier said than done. It doesn't come easily for most of us.

Have you ever struggled forgiving someone?
How could you forgive when you are not ready?
How could you forgive when you're lost, confused, or living in constant fear?

It is important to remember, even when you feel it's impossible to forgive, there are ways to get moving. Here are some practical tips you can follow when you struggle to forgive:

- **Give yourself some space**
  Our environment has a huge impact on the decisions we make. If you're surrounded by people that drain your energy, or live in a negative place, the choices you make will produce undesirable outcomes. Every relationship has its ups and downs, and there may be times when you feel like you need space. It is important to remember that you only have a limited amount of energy each day, so use it wisely.

- **Give yourself time to heal**
  Forgiveness is a gift for yourself. When you forgive, it is more for "YOU" than for others. Forgiveness is a process and takes time. It is not a one-time event. If you are continually struggling with getting hurt over and over, it's

almost impossible to have the right mindset to forgive. Sometimes you need to step back if pain existed for a long time. The pain may have created constant anxiety, emotional problems, or fears of the future. Sometimes, it is essential to allow yourself to go through the emotions.

Focus on taking one step at a time. Taking time for yourself will enable you to renew, heal, and create reserves of energy and peace.

- **Pray or meditate**

    Forgiveness is returning to God the right to take care of justice. By refusing to transfer the right for exact punishment or revenge, we are telling God we don't trust him to take care of matters. In times of desperation, I turned to prayer. Meditation can offer this same sense of giving control to the universe so that you no longer need to carry that burden.

You may be in the same place, struggling to decide to forgive. Allow yourself to have the time, space, and resources you need to heal. Remember, for forgiveness happen; you have to be willing and decide to forgive.

Nancy Colier LCSW, Rev, a psychotherapist, interfaith minister, author, and relationship coach has written on her blog the following article about forgiveness:

Forgiveness is Not Saying:
- You were not hurt by what the other person did.
- Your pain is gone.
- You are back to being the person you were before it happened.
- Life can now pick up where you left off; you feel the way you did before, as if what happened never happened.
- You no longer believe the other person was responsible for causing harm.
- You excuse the other person's behavior.

Rose Sweet, writer on FocusOnTheFamily.com, posted an interesting article about forgiveness and restoration.

The first step to understanding forgiveness is learning what it is and isn't. The next step is giving yourself permission to forgive and forget, letting go of the bitterness while remembering very clearly your rights to healthy boundaries.

Granting Forgiveness

- **Forgiveness is not letting the offense recur again and again.** We don't have to tolerate, nor should we keep ourselves open to, lack of respect or any form of abuse.
- **Forgiveness does not mean we have to revert to being the victim.** Forgiving is not saying, "What you did was okay, so go ahead and walk all over me." Nor is it playing the martyr, enjoying the performance of forgiving people because it perpetuates our victim role.

- **Forgiveness is not the same as reconciling.** We can forgive someone even if we never can get along with him again.
- **Forgetting does not mean denying reality or ignoring repeated offenses.** Some people are obnoxious, mean-spirited, apathetic, or unreliable. They never will change. We need to change the way we respond to them and quit expecting them to be different.
- **Forgiveness is not based on others' actions but on our attitude.** People will continue to hurt us through life. We either can look outward at them or stay stuck and angry, or we can begin to keep our minds on our loving relationship with God, knowing and trusting in what is good.
- **We don't always have to tell them we have forgiven them.** Self-righteously announcing our gracious forgiveness to someone who has not asked to be forgiven may be a manipulation to make them feel guilty. It also is a form of pride.
- **Withholding forgiveness is a refusal to let go of perceived power.** We can feel powerful when the offender is in need of forgiveness and only we can give it. We may fear going back to being powerless if we forgive.
- **We might forgive too quickly to avoid pain or to manipulate the situation.** Forgiveness releases pain and frees us from focusing on the other person. Too often when we're in the midst of the turmoil after a divorce, we desperately look for a quick fix to make it all go away. Some women want to "hurry up" and forgive so the pain will end, or so they can get along with the other person. We have to

be careful not to simply cover our wounds and retard the healing process.
- **We might be pressured into false forgiveness before we are ready.** When we feel obligated or we forgive just so others will still like us, accept us, or not think badly of us, it's not true forgiveness — it's a performance to avoid rejection. Give yourself permission to do it right. Maybe all you can offer today is, "I want to forgive you, but right now I'm struggling emotionally. I promise I will work on it."
- **Forgiveness starts with a mental decision.** The emotional part of forgiveness is finally being able to let go of the resentment. Emotional healing may or may not follow quickly after we forgive.

Over to you:

Forgiving may be easier said than done. Here are some questions you can use as a guideline as you work on the area of forgiveness:

1. Is there anybody who has hurt you?
2. Have you released forgiveness?
3. Are you ready to forgive?
4. Are you ready to forgive yourself?

If not, take your time and do what's needed to be in that position. Each person will forgive at his or her own pace. Remember, to be 100% ready is not possible at all times.

You have a choice; it's up to you to make that choice. You can stay bitter and resentful, or you can take one step at a time towards living in the present and creating the happy life you desire. When you make a decision, the rest follows.

Here are some affirmations you can use if you are having a hard time to let go or are struggling to forgive. Say them out loud at least once a day and meditate on them throughout the day and night.

- I am at peace.
- I am forgiven, I am free.
- I forgive others and myself.
- I forgive myself for being imperfect like everybody else. However, I still manage to live the best life I can.
- I love and accept myself, fully and unconditionally.
- I am letting go of all the anger and frustration.
- Every day is a new opportunity to start over and be the best version of myself.
- The past is over, so it has no power now. The thoughts of this moment create my future.
- I'm ready to be healed. I'm willing to forgive. All is well.

Read the meditation below. Take a moment to meditate and confess this with an open heart and mind.

Even if you are skeptical, or not 100% sure you want to do this, be open to try, and you're on your way to releasing forgiveness:

I am hurt badly, and I don't know how to do this. But I'm taking the first step; I'm now willing to forgive. I'm releasing all the hatred, anger, pain, trauma into your hands, and asking you to release forgiveness in me. The past is gone. I live in the present. I'm embracing forgiveness for myself and the people who caused me pain and harmed me. Today is a new opportunity to start over and be the best version of myself. I am healed, I am forgiven, I am at peace, I am free.

CHAPTER 8
BE READY TO RECEIVE

The truth is revealed when you are ready to receive it when you need it in order to move forward to take the next step in your journey. To move on toward your destiny.
— *Alyson Noel*

What do you want in life?

Wealth, power, fame, relationships, a healthy body, talent, businesses, fancy cars, a big house, the latest gadgets, travel, and more?

Are you ready to receive what you ask for?
What are you willing to sacrifice to get what you desire?
How prepared are you to receive what you want?

Saying you want something and becoming the person who is ready to receive is different.

Imagine if you get the promotion you've been asking for. What if it requires more time traveling away from your family? If you have your own family, how will your partner or kids adjust to the situation?

If you are looking for a relationship or wanted to settle down with someone, visualize that you find them. Are you ready to open up and to trust? Are you open to sharing your emotions, finances, dreams, and other aspects of your life with him/her? Are you willing to put your partner first before your favorite activities, sports or movies?

If you wanted to have kids, have you asked if your partner is ready? Have you considered the chores and duties involved with raising your own kids?

As humans, we are wired to want more, to seek growth and progress, which forms the underlying framework for development. But are we ready to receive? Do we have the right mindset and character to support what we are asking for?

You only get out what you put in

My journey started with a desire for wanting a better life instead of being in a toxic environment for the rest of my life. If I didn't take any action to change things, I would never be ready to receive what I wanted.

After almost three months of my journey, I received many offers in my career and had grown in all aspects of my life. During that time, I had dreamt, decided to change, and followed my desires. I considered my options, then acted. I left my family, saved enough money to support myself, quit my comfortable job, took my chances in a foreign land, and applied for jobs all day long. I stepped out of my comfort zone.

I dealt with rejection, pain, and being abused at home. When I stepped out of my comfort zone, I allowed myself to be more exposed to rejection and pain in the world.

I was rejected several times, not only in my job hunting but even trying to stay longer in the country. Eventually, all the rejection, pain, and loss I'd experienced became the primary motivator for my actions. It stretched me out and built the character I needed before I received what I wanted.

The Big Day

I still remember the day I received great news all at once. First thing in the morning, I got a job offer at a call center with the salary I asked. Second, I received a call. Another job offer from a multinational company in Singapore. The contract included above-average pay, triple the income of my last job. The first two months would be based in Canada, all expenses paid. Third, another call from my niece, who told me that she received my employment certification. I could come back anytime. I was granted two years to stay in Singapore and apply for other jobs without worrying anymore about extending the visa pass.

The price of success is hard work, dedication to the job at hand, and the determination that whether we win or lose, we have applied the best of ourselves to the task at hand."
- *Vince Lombardi*

Success necessitates sacrifice. It all pays off in the end.

When you have given your best to pursue what you want, even if you didn't get it, there is nothing to be ashamed of. If you get what you wanted, it is usually more than what you expected. You're overjoyed. It's indescribable.

Thoughts to Ponder:

You may have dreams and ambitions in life.
You give your best but it still not enough. No matter how hard you try, it feels impossible. You are not getting what you want.

Don't lose hope. His ways are better than ours. It is tough to go on this ride by yourself. Lean on Him. You will realize "Not yet" doesn't mean "Denial" at all times.

Sometimes, you must go through this journey. It makes your character stronger. It helps you know yourself better. When the right time comes, you will understand the reason why.

The journey you're going through prepares you for your breakthrough.

Over to you:

Set aside a block of time to work through the following questions.

1. What is the one thing you've been asking for?

2. Are you ready to receive it?

If you haven't received it yet, what do you think is stopping you from getting it? Is there any aspect of your life you need to revisit?

CHAPTER 9
SEASONS OF LIFE

Seasons come, seasons go, seasons change, but the lessons remain. You can't force a season to last if its time has passed. Happiness is loving every season for different reasons. Embrace the season you're in, and when it's time to let go, embrace your chance to begin again.
- Mandy Hale

Just like in some countries where they have winter, spring, summer or fall, or in some places where they have summer and rainy seasons, your life has its seasons.

In summer, we get so excited and plan to be outside most of the time. In the winter, or on rainy days, it gets dark and we prefer to just stay cozy inside at home. Similar to our lives, there are times to plant seeds and to harvest, to go through difficulties or to celebrate.

What season of life are you in?

After forgiving my father, I realized how the harvest season came into my life. I mentioned in the previous chapter, the multiple offers I received, which were more than I expected. I picked the best option based on what I needed most at that time. I accepted the job offer in Singapore.

My first day on the job was not a typical first day in the office; I flew to Canada for two months of training. Although it was all expenses paid, I had to use my credit card and money first before I was reimbursed. The challenge: I lent money to others, maxed out my credit card, and used up my savings. I was too shy to ask others to pay me back even when I needed it. Puzzled about what to do, I shared my situation with my mom and asked for her opinion. I had the job offer, flight ticket and itineraries but didn't have any money left for an allowance or in case of emergency.

I knew I shouldn't lend money. I only had enough to cover my expenses. But I did because I didn't know how to say "No." Without question or hesitation, my mom wired me some cash. I knew she didn't have her own money since my dad came back home, so I asked where she got it from.

"Don't you remember the money you gave me every time you got paid before? I saved It all," she said.

I had given it to her a while back because I wanted her to enjoy it. I didn't know she saved it all. And then she gave it all back to me knowing that I needed it more.

That moment reminded me of my purpose. I am here with the mission to grow in all aspects of my life and to help my family to have a better life. The seeds I'd sown became available to me, when I needed them the most, in my harvest time.

There are times when we get so caught up with the moment, we enjoy the experience, being around the new people we meet. Embracing new experiences. However, never forget where you came from and why you are where you are at in the first place.

Like the seasons of life, enjoy whatever season you're in but don't forget the other seasons you've been through.

It is only when we embrace every season of our lives fully, and stop resisting; we become more alive. As you embrace the current season of your life, don't waste the other seasons that passed, the winter time of your life, the pain and suffering you've been through.

The winter season or rainy days may feel like forever. You may be wondering, how long will it last? Will it be over soon, can I still make it?

If you're going through tough times, and feel like giving up, ask and seek God to give you the strength, the right people and resources you need to keep going. It's hard to walk alone in the dark moments of our lives. It's harder when we walk with the wrong people, but with God's wisdom, and the right support, you'll be amazed about what will happen next.

During the right season, it will make more sense. You'll never know how your experience could be a blessing to others.

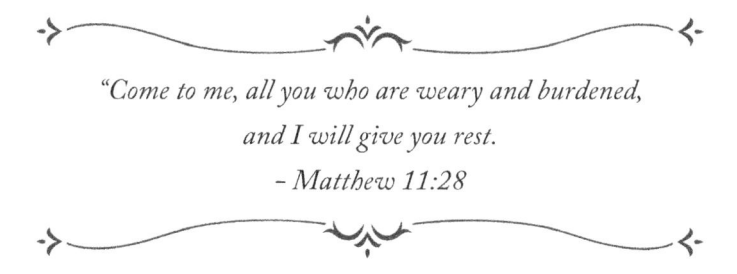

"Come to me, all you who are weary and burdened, and I will give you rest.
- Matthew 11:28

Understanding the seasons of life

I was on a monthly salary in the job I accepted. It was my first job in Singapore, and the first two months were based in Canada. The money I got from my mom was only good for a few weeks. Once the pesos were converted to Canadian dollars, it wasn't that much. Although everything was covered on my trip: the food, transportation, accommodation, everything, I had to request the reimbursement first and it usually took a month to get it back.

I had no idea what would happen next, but I knew one thing for sure, God was with me. He was protecting me every single step I took.

One afternoon, I logged into my computer and checked my online bank account. Surprisingly, there were a few thousand dollars credited to it.

"Wow, I thought I wasn't supposed to get any pay yet!" I exclaimed. Two minutes later, I received an email.

"Hi Marge,

I would like to notify you that there was some glitch with the payment for this cut-off. Someone's pay was deposited to your account. There was confusion between you and another lady in the company. Both of you have the same first five characters. Ma.Victoria, is the same as yours, Ma. Virginia. Her payment went to your account, but you don't have to do anything on your end. Payroll will make the adjustment in the next cut off. I just wanted you to be aware of this."

Isn't that amazing?

What fascinated me during harvest season was that, no matter what obstacles I encountered, I got the help and resources needed to keep going. I didn't have to look for it like I did in the winter time; it just keeps flowing.

Although everything that I have done in the past is all part of the process to be where I'm at today, moving from the Philippines to Singapore opened-up many possibilities in my life.

It allowed me to experience faith, hope, peace, love, joy and forgiveness. By the time I got the job I had desired, the fear of stepping into the unknown had vanished. It wasn't because I got the job; it was because of the character I developed throughout my experiences. Everything I've learned and the people who have helped shape me into the person I am today.

I learned to fully trust God to be with me as I achieved each goal. I faced bumps in the road and kept standing. I always knew I had his helping hands throughout my journey.

I was in the winter season for a long time when I was dealing with pain in my family. It wasn't days, weeks, a year, it was almost a decade of my life. Even when I took my chance in Singapore as a tourist, I still encountered difficulties. But going through those challenges in my life, allowed me to embrace each season and appreciate life more than I could ever imagine.

Over to you:

Take some time to reflect on below verses. As you go through it, imagine the seasons of life you've been through and you'll be facing.

How did you face each season? Did you embrace it? Will you embrace it this time?

To everything, there is a season,
and a time to every purpose under the heaven:
A time to be born, a time to die;
a time to plant, and a time to pluck up that which is planted;
A time to kill, and a time to heal;
a time to break down, and a time to build up;
A time to weep, and a time to laugh;
a time to mourn, and a time to dance;
A time to cast away stones, and a time to gather stones together;
a time to embrace, and a time to refrain from embracing;
A time to get, and a time to lose;
a time to keep, and a time to cast away;
A time to rend, and a time to sew;
a time to keep silence, and a time to speak;
A time to love, and a time to hate;
A time of war, and a time of peace.
- Ecclesiastes 3:1-8

CHAPTER 10
GIVING BACK TO OTHERS

We make a living by what we get. We make a life by what we give.
- Winston S. Churchill

Giving is the highest expression of potency. Giving is more joyous than receiving, not because it is a deprivation, but because in the act of giving lies the expression of my aliveness.
- Erich Fromm

The number of tourists exploring jobs and opportunities continues to increase every year. One of the challenges that people abroad face is homesickness — a feeling of longing for one's home over time.

Some factors that contribute to it are adjusting to a new environment, culture, language, and the list could go on and on. Individuals also put a lot of pressure on themselves to get a job quickly to provide for their family. Without any support, it could lead to anxiety, depression, withdrawn behavior, or worse.

I have experienced this challenging situation. I was fortunate to get some support during those times when I felt discouraged and defeated. Without the help that I received from the people around me, I'm not sure if I would have survived those tough times.

Since I made my decision to step into the unknown, I mourned and suffered as I went through life. But when I met people that showed love, support, and kindness without expecting anything in return, it made me realize I'm not alone. I got encouraged, and it fuelled me to pursue my dreams and desires.

Suffering produces endurance. Endurance produces character. Character produces hope.

It strengthened my faith in God and myself. It made me stronger than ever before. And when the time to reap came, I couldn't contain my joy; it was overflowing. I asked for little but received a hundredfold in return. I was lost but now found meaning in life. I experienced all of this because of my mom's kindness and the kindness of random people I met in my life. I was overwhelmed with all the blessings I received and simply couldn't avoid giving back to others.

I got involved with a community who assisted newcomers to Singapore. Together, we shared our experiences and encouraged them. I helped by providing tools to be more effective in job hunting and assisted them in establishing a social and professional network.

One of the greatest feelings I had was to be part of the dreams being fulfilled and the lives being transformed for the people I met in my journey.

Here are some inspiring stories about how a random act of kindness lead to something big in the lives of others.

One random act of kindness can make a difference

It was early one Sunday morning when I met Jenn. Similar to what I did, she took a leap of faith to quit her job in the Philippines for better opportunities in a foreign land. Her father was a pastor of a growing church. Aside from helping her family, she wanted to help her local church in funding and expanding its mission.

The first time we met, I asked Jenn to join me together with the youth group for lunch. She said she wasn't hungry but would love to mingle around. It was four of us at that time, Sheryl, Jay, Jenn, and me. I asked what she wanted for lunch and offered to pay for it. I was glad she had joined us. We all had our burger meals and enjoyed the moment. Jenn didn't talk a lot but responded to questions we asked and observed the group. As time went by, Jenn became comfortable hanging out with the rest of the youth group and me. We became good friends and continued to stay in touch to encourage one another.

On my 25th birthday, I had a simple celebration. I didn't want to have a big party because I missed my family. Instead, I went to the park with my four friends. Jenn was one of them, who at that time, already had a stable job and worked as a manager in a big restaurant.

Jenn said, "Marge, do you remember the first time we met? When I first joined you guys at one of the Sunday services, and you paid for my lunch. What you didn't know was that I was broke at that time. I had gone through all my savings. I had no idea where to get my next meal. That burger meal you got for me was an answered prayer. I had a few bites and saved the rest for the next few days."

It's incredible how the simple things we do, can make a difference in the lives of others. **Sometimes, you don't understand why you do things, but there is something inside of you saying, "just do it!". At the right time, the real purpose behind it will be revealed to you.**

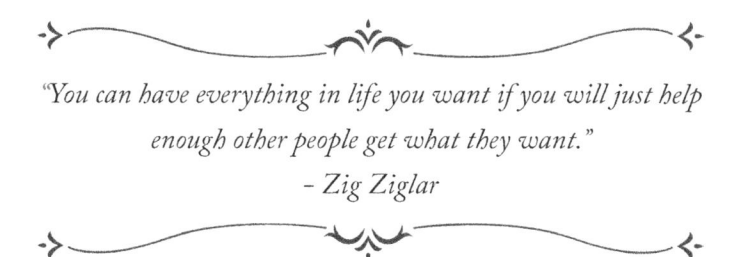

> *"You can have everything in life you want if you will just help enough other people get what they want."*
> *- Zig Ziglar*

Brook was an international student in the Engineering program at Lakehead University in Thunder Bay, Ontario. He came from China and did his internship at the company I was working for. I had the opportunity to mentor him as he reported to me at the time. During some of our one-on-one sessions, he shared some of his challenges as an immigrant, aside from the projects we collaborated on. Having this common ground, I shared some of my experiences as I moved to different countries and provided guidelines on adjusting to the culture and lifestyle.

Brook aspired to become a developer. Even though we badly wanted him for our test team, we supported and assisted him in achieving his desire. He eventually moved to the Ottawa office where he got a developer role. We remained good friends and kept in touch.

In 2014 he wrote, "I would like to say thank you again. Without you, I'm sure my coop term would be a different one. Your thoughts and teaching, I will remember forever. I will always appreciate your kindness and patience."

Brook continues to work as a developer. He sponsored his wife to come to Canada, and they are finally together and settled down in Ottawa. He is also now helping some of his friends coming from China to adjust to the culture in Canada.

> "Wherever there is a human in need, there is an opportunity for kindness and to make a difference."
> - Kevin Heath

I remember my mentor GJ shared this story. While she was praying, she was prompted to visit one of her friends; she hadn't seen her for a long time. She brought some flowers and went directly to visit her. She found out that her friend battled depression and wanted to commit suicide. When she received the flowers and saw GJ's present, she was deeply moved and felt loved. She shared her struggles, and together, they looked for ways to get the support she needed.

With a small action, you can save someone's life.

> "Kindness is giving hope to those who think they are all alone in this world."
> - RAKtivist

As my income multiplied, I became fascinated by how I could do more for others, especially for my family.

One time, I called my mom. I found out that she was doing laundry for our family by hand. The washing machine had stopped working – not surprising as it was 15 years old. I didn't bother asking them to repair it. The same thing had happened to their fridge. They knew it needed to be replaced, but it would take some time before they could save the money needed.

They had never asked me for help, but right away, I wired money into their account. The next day, I asked them to check their bank account. I told them to use the money to get a new fridge, washing machine, and any other appliances they needed. My mom was surprised and with tears in her eyes said that it had saved her back and body from all the pain of doing the laundry by hand.

Small things we do make a huge difference in the lives of others.

Things to watch out for:

Although giving back sounds like a good act and comes naturally for others, it is important to have clarity on your intention and to get equipped in this area.

If your intention is good and for the right cause, you can make a difference in the lives of others and yourself. **Understanding the boundaries will stop others from taking advantage of you.**

As I have run my race, I have met people who question giving. If I look at them, they would rather spend their money on things they don't need, instead of making a difference in someone else's life. Sometimes, this group of people is also the same ones who expect you to lend them your resources, like time, money and energy if they run out.

One of the pastors I met in Malaysia told me, **"Give your heart but keep your brain."** It's a great motto to remember. As you get encouraged to keep giving back to others, it is vital to be aware that sometimes, others can use your kindness to take advantage of you.

There were other groups of people I met on my journey that could have taken advantage of me easily, if I hadn't learned to draw the line. I could have lost my time, energy, and other resources.

As you continue to achieve your goals and become financially blessed, it is important to be a good steward as well. **You are where you are because of what you have put in. Watch out for others who could pull you down and steal what you have sown.** I can't emphasize more how important this point is. Drawing boundaries is necessary to protect yourself.

You may have chosen to focus on your side hustle, delayed several trips, said no to several events while everyone else was having fun. They enjoyed their favorite TV shows, spent without thinking of the future, often expecting someone to lend them money or provide for them. Who do you think would reach their goal, you or them?

Here are some tips you could use to stop letting others take advantage of you when you are giving:

- When you give back to others, it must come from your desire.
  If you don't have peace in your heart, or you feel obligated or guilty, it is not the best way to give.
- Pray to God. Ask for wisdom.
- Keep your brain, and give with your heart
  Observe the lifestyle of the people around you and make a wise decision. Learn the importance of saying "No." This will be discussed more in chapter 12.
- Remember that you can't give what you don't have.
  If you give something you don't have, you are stealing from yourself. If you budget all the money for the month and nothing extra is left, should you lend money to someone?
- Don't lend something you can't afford to lose.
- Equip yourself
  A great book to read about giving back to others is The Paradox of Generosity: Giving, We Receive; Grasping We Lose. A well-researched book that states that the wealth of evidence reveals a consistent link between demonstrating generosity and living a better life: generous people are happier, suffer fewer illnesses and injuries, live with a greater sense of purpose, and experience less depression.

Over to you:

Set aside a block of time to work through the following questions.

1. What's one Act of Kindness have done today?

    If you haven't done one yet, what are you waiting for?
    If you already did, how does it feel?

    Remember, nothing is stopping you from doing less if you don't feel fulfilled. If you feel exhausted or you need a break, how about considering some kindness to your self?

Here are some tips you could use to start with:

- Find opportunities to give compliments. It costs nothing, takes no time, and could make someone's entire day. Don't just think about it. Say it.
- Find ways to tell people that you care.
    It doesn't matter how you do it - it only matters that you do it. You can say it, write it, tweet it, or deliver the message in person. Make a choice every day to tell, offer, thank, encourage, inspire, and let others know you notice and believe in them.
- Hold the door open for someone

An excellent site to visit that talks about One Act of Kindness: https://www.bradaronson.com/acts-of-kindness/

CHAPTER 11
ACHIEVING YOUR GOALS AND SETTING NEW ONES

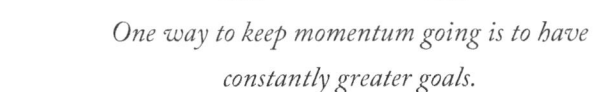

One way to keep momentum going is to have constantly greater goals.
– Michael Korda

How many dreams have you made come true in your life? How many skills have you acquired since childhood?

Dreams of:
- getting the toy you wanted for Christmas or on your birthday
- learning new skills like swimming, biking, dancing, cooking
- finishing elementary school
- exploring different places with your mom and dad
- celebrating parties with friends

Think of how it made you feel when you got these dreams fulfilled when you were little. Then you started aiming for bigger ones like:
- Finishing secondary school
- Completing a college or university degree
- Getting your dream job
- Getting your first paycheque
- Meeting your dream partner
- Getting married and having kids
- Traveling
- Having your own house, car, cellphone, tablet and many other material things you could think of
- Getting your first investment (stocks, investment properties, other commodities)
- Advancing your career
- Having a side hustle
- Having your own business

Since you were young, have you noticed how many dreams you have you accomplished in your life? Isn't that amazing?

With those dreams, some of them came true, and some did not. As I reflect upon my life, and as I get older, I realize that it is easier to set aside many of my dreams. As my commitments increased, the desire to dream again and pursue them seemed impossible.

When I was a child, I had simple ideas, and every time I achieved it, I was overjoyed.

My biggest dream, since I was young, was to have a better life. I had other dreams, like learning to dance, perform, graduate from elementary school, high school, and to complete my university degree. I dreamt of getting my first princess toy, cellphone, laptop, my first job, my first house, car, and many more things. Few dreams were difficult to achieve.

Then my life circumstances changed, I started working, got married, had kids. I had more commitments in life. I realized my unfulfilled dreams were still in my heart but pursuing them would require more effort on my part. I had to know which ones to prioritize. With the busy routine of my family, job, and other things I loved to do, I struggled to find the balance. If I pushed myself to do it all at once, I could not have had any rest or even sleep.

I had some demanding dreams: continuously investing in real estate, getting my real estate license, writing books, coaching, online businesses, reading more, having a clean house and spending more time with my family, especially with my little kids. Aside from my new commitments in life, I'm still a daughter of my parents, a friend, and I have myself to take care of.

Dreams keep evolving based on our life circumstances. As you realize some, there are new ones that will come to mind. But some remain in your heart until you take the time to pursue them.

As my commitments grew, managing my time became more challenging. But despite obligations and increasing responsibilities, I'd find ways to pursue and continue to fulfill my dreams without compromising what mattered most in my life. It is not easy, but doable.

Here are some guidelines to help you pursue your dreams, despite the commitments you may have:

1. KNOW YOUR PRIORITIES

In one of Oprah's Life class shows, relationship expert Iyania Vanzant said, "It is not selfish to put yourself first, it is Self-Full. You want to run with a cup full to be of great service to others. You have to be good to yourself first if you want to be of service in life. How you treat yourself is how you treat God, because you are the representation of God in your life. So, when you put yourself last, you put God last. Remember, people violate you when you don't have clear boundaries."

If all you do is put everybody else's life ahead of your own, you set aside all your dreams and ambitions. This doesn't do a favor to yourself or anyone else. One day, the people you care for will go on with their own lives and you will wonder what to do next or lament where you went. Trying to make everyone happy can make you miserable in the long run.

Your life is valuable to live like everyone else.

It is important to remember that you don't have to give up everything to put yourself first. Decide to set aside some time for yourself, include it in your priorities and align it with your circumstances. For example, the commitment you need to give to your kids when they are little, and when they are teenagers, is different. This doesn't mean you can't start working on what you want. You need to have clarity about what you can do now.

When I started working on my real estate license, my eldest child was two years old, and I was pregnant with my second one. I had a fulltime job in IT, and on weekends, I served in a kid's ministry. I was also a wife, mother, daughter, friend, an employee with different commitments and had hobbies and goals in life.

Knowing my priorities allowed me to understand what kind of commitment I could give in pursuit of the rest of my dreams. I always knew my family came first, but I wanted to get my real estate license for my personal and my family's investments. It was six courses that needed to be completed within 18 months of enrollment. Knowing I had a strong desire to get my license, I made a commitment to make it happen, which also required some sacrifices. When everybody was asleep, I spent an hour studying. I had to say no to social media and limit social events for a certain amount of time.

By the time my second daughter was born, I had completed all the courses needed and got my license. I joined a team where I learned a tremendous amount. After a few months of doing it, I recognized that doing it full time would be challenging with everything I had on my plate, but it didn't stop me from learning what I could.

In less than six months after I got my license, I had a stronger understanding of the local real estate market, which allowed me to be more creative in increasing our real estate investments, gaining connections with skilled tradespeople and most of all, developing a new skill set.

When you know why you do things, and you are clear with your priorities, you will continue to progress towards achieving your goals, no matter how big they are.

It doesn't matter what others say if **you** know your purpose. One step at a time towards your goal will eventually bring you there. It's the consistent action that you do every day that matters. Instead of waiting for when it is the next best time, like when your kids grow up or the next client comes, ask yourself, what if tomorrow never comes? What if you only have today? What can you do now to make it happen? Just do it! Take action!

Remember, we're only guaranteed today, so stop waiting for tomorrow.

2. MAKE TIME FOR WHAT MATTERS MOST

The very first thing to do is to get rid of the limiting belief that "there is never enough time." Entertaining this thought programmed your mind to be defeated before you even got started. This belief usually comes from living a distracted life, where you are constantly interrupted by urgent things around you. In the end, we feel that we are living an unfulfilled, incomplete, dissatisfied, and unhappy life.

Unconsciously, you find yourself jumping from one task to another without applying the right priorities in your life. I experienced this when I saw myself working after office hours, instead of pursuing my other goals like reading books or working on a business. I was taking work calls early in the morning, around 6:00 am when my kids were still asleep. I jumped to other tasks related to my projects when I had some availability. The same thing happened when I chose to watch movies or turned to Facebook or Instagram for a couple of hours and didn't have time to read, write, go to classes, seminars or conferences. There was simply no time to improve myself. It was only when I took some time to identify what matters most in my life when I learned to plan my schedule based on my priorities, that amazing thing happened!

Despite the commitments I had, I started achieving my goals and continued to set new ones. I learned to let go and say "No" without guilt and lived life by design, not by default.

We all have the same 24 hours in a day. Take time to solidify your priorities in life. Take action by taking one small step at a time.

Remember, what separates the doer and the dreamer is the ability to follow through. Doers do what is needed to get what they want. There's more than enough time for what matters most.

> *"There is never enough time to do everything, but there is always enough time to do the most important thing."*
> - Brian Tracy

3. BUILD A SUPPORT TEAM

Surround yourself with the right people. As John Maxwell wrote in Roadmap for success: "The greater the dream, the greater the people who will be attracted to you. But that alone isn't enough. You need to make sure they are compatible with you."

Before you begin looking at the qualities that make a person right for joining you on your journey, you need to ask yourself these three questions:

First: Does this person want to go?
Second: Is this person able to go?
Third: Can this person make the trip without me?

Surrounding yourself with the right people changes everything. Especially nowadays, where we have online access, there is no limit to how you can connect with others. Spend most of your time with the people you want to be with.

4. HAVE A GOAL SETTING SYSTEM IN PLACE

Find a goal setting technique that would work for you and stick to it!

There are different techniques for goal setting; the classics are the S.M.A.R.T goal, the One Thing planner, Vision Board or baby steps; you just need to find the one that works best for you.

An excellent article that talks about different systems: https://marketingartfully.com/5-goal-setting-systems/

Over to you:

Set aside a block of time to work through the following questions.

1. What was the last dream you achieved?
2. What are the other dreams you would like to pursue next?
3. Out of those dreams, what is that one dream you started working or would like to achieve first?
4. When will you start working on it?
5. What's your timeline to get it done?
6. Who's your support group?

CHAPTER 12
INVEST IN YOURSELF

Investing in yourself is the best investment you will ever make. It will not only improve your life, but it will also improve the lives of all those around you.
– Robin S. Sharma

When was the last time you invested in yourself?

When I ask this question, I don't mean those times when you were watching your favorite TV show or treating yourself with a nice meal. I mean something you've done for yourself where you learned, have grown in a way that would help you become the person you wanted to be.

If you can't remember when, then it's time to be reminded of the most significant investment you missed out on. Taking time to improve on yourself, skills, and what you can offer to the world can be one of the most profitable decisions you'll ever make.

It's been almost twenty years since I decided that I would have a better life. I felt like I was living in survival mode and wanted a change. I started by making small changes, taking one step at a time to invest in myself.

Growing up in a dysfunctional family was very toxic. But accepting what I couldn't control and focusing on what I could, helped me to progress in life. By being consistent in making small changes for my personal growth, it allowed me to boost my confidence, build resilience, gain inner strength, and achieved a better life. It made me accomplish the dreams and desires I had, not only for myself but also for others.

I read tons of books and other resources that contributed to my growth. I committed to reading at least fifteen minutes every day, and my knowledge continued to grow. The small steps I took constantly when I was in my early twenties paid off. They allowed me to go to different places, strengthen my character, and guided me in my decisions in life. Right now, I can afford to hire coaches and go to many seminars, but when I started my journey, I relied on the free resources available around me.

Investing in yourself would probably be the last thing you could think if you're going through tough times. But, if you want to change where you are at, you need to decide to change where you are going.

Don't worry about how to get there. Focus on taking one step at a time. You'll be amazed by how the next steps will be revealed to you once you act consistently on improving yourself.

Each step you take, will help you to look at the bright side despite dark circumstances. Instead of asking, what did I do wrong to get stuck in the situation, you'll learn to ask better questions like what is the one thing I can do to make the situation better?

As novelist Leo Tolstoy said, *"Everyone thinks of changing the world, but no one thinks of changing himself."*

If you are committed to improving your life, Investment in Yourself is one of the most profitable decisions you could ever make.

If you don't invest in yourself, who else will?

You may feel lucky if your employer paid for your training or seminars, but is that what you really want to do? For some, it helps, but there are other aspects of your life where you need to grow. No one can give everything to you. The cold truth is, you need to do the work. It must start within **You.**

There's no limit on what you can achieve, where you can go, or who you could become if you do the work needed to make things happen. Start investing in yourself. It is the one decision that has been mastered by many successful people throughout history.

Tony Robbins grew up poor, with a troubled childhood. His mom was an alcoholic and he had four different fathers. He started as a broke janitor. He saved a week's worth of pay and then spent it in a way that changed his life. At seventeen, he spent a week's salary on a Jim Rohn seminar. Rohn helped Robbins develop a coaching style that made him famous by his mid-20s. He is now known as the nation's top life and business strategist.

J.K. Rowling, the author of the much-loved series of seven Harry Potter novels, had the idea of the characters while she was delayed on a train traveling from Manchester to London King's Cross in 1990. Before creating the series, she was clinically depressed. She spent the next few years struggling to meet ends meet. She was jobless, a lone parent, and broke. She even contemplated suicide. Luckily, she used her writing as an outlet for her pain. The idea for the Harry Potter series had come to her years before and she had worked on a few chapters in Portugal, but she only really found her momentum when she was back in the UK.

Warren Buffet said, "Ultimately, there's one investment that supersedes all others: Invest in yourself. Nobody can take away what you've got in yourself, and everybody has potential they haven't used yet."

One of his first investments was in his early adulthood when he signed up for a $100 Dale Carnegie public speaking course that he said changed his life.

"I was terrified of public speaking when I was young. I couldn't do it," he said.

Warren Buffett is now a billionaire investor, speaker, and philanthropist. He is noted for his adherence to value investing and for his frugality despite his immense wealth.

These people have left lasting marks in history. What they have in common is the desire to improve their lives and invest in themselves.

No one can guarantee what tomorrow could bring. But whatever you put into YOU now would serve as a foundation for what you will create.

No matter what circumstances you are in, you have the greatest asset to make it better. You have in you the most important element to succeed. You, and only you, have to be proactive enough to take that responsibility.

Here are some practical ways to start investing in yourself to create a better version of you:

1. Continuous Growth

Complacency kills growth. If you want to succeed in what you do, you need to grow. *John Maxwell said, "Continual growth has its difficult moments as well as rewarding ones. If your current circumstances do nothing to help you grow, you're going to have a hard time enlarging yourself to reach your potential."*

Listed below are some key ways for continuous growth:

- **Read or listen to the right content to grow and achieve.** Read or listen to resources (blogs, books/audiobooks, magazines, etc.) to build your knowledge and expertise in any area.

- **Surround yourself with the people that inspire you or create an environment that will allow you to grow.** The people around you have a significant impact on your life. Surround yourself with people you can grow with. This may be challenging in some situations, like with my own experiences, coming from abuse and dysfunctional family. Don't allow the situation to stop you. You can use the power of books, social media, or even think of people you know that inspire you to create a growth environment.

- **Get an accountability group/partner**
  You can join classes, seminars, mastermind groups or other related events to find like-minded people that will inspire, encourage and hold you accountable.

- **Serve**
  Humans are wired for helping others, when you serve you are not only helping others but also allowing yourself to grow.

  As Warren Buffett said: "It's better to hang out with people better than you. Pick out associates whose behavior is better than yours and you'll drift in that direction."

- **Explore, dream, discover**
  A famous quote from H. Jackson Brown Jr., *P.S. I Love You,* explained it well, "Twenty years from now you will be more disappointed by the things that you didn't do than by the ones you did do. So throw off the bowlines. Sail away from the safe harbor. Catch the trade winds in your sails. Explore. Dream. Discover."

2. **Improve Self-awareness**

Self-awareness is awareness of your actions, your emotions, and your life. Knowing and understanding ourselves is a powerful guide for living our best life. Improving our self-awareness builds confidence to help direct us on our life's path. Listed below are some tips you could use to develop this area:

- **Set aside a time for yourself to develop daily self-reflection.**
  You could start with 15 minutes and start writing/journaling your thoughts. Reflect on it by the end of the day or the end of the week. This will help you see yourself from a different perspective. It would also allow you to make necessary adjustments.

- **Practice mindfulness**
  You can start this by being fully present at the moment. Wherever you are, give your 100% focus in the situation. It is easy to get distracted with cool gadgets and technology we have nowadays. If you want to develop self-awareness, start working on being mindful.

- **Set boundaries**
  Know when to say No and Yes without feeling guilty. Sometimes saying NO is just as important as saying YES. You must learn to say YES and NO to the right things and create boundaries within your life. And just because you say NO to something doesn't make you are a bad person.

  Saying Yes to one thing, ultimately is the same as saying No to another. Saying No makes time for opportunities for you to focus on things you want to accomplish.

3. Release Creativity

Creativity is the use of the imagination or original ideas, especially in the production of artistic work. It gives us a sense of purpose above and beyond our daily task.

A 2010 review published in the American Journal of Public Health called The Connection Between Art, Healing, and Public Health: A Review of Current Literature, aimed to do just that—measure how creative practices enhance health and wellbeing. Their findings revealed strong connections between art and mental health as well as physical health benefits. Specifically, the researchers found out how creativity affects the brain and body, leading to benefits like increased mood, decreased anxiety, heightened cognitive function, reduced risk of chronic illnesses and improved immune health.

Creativity is about letting go. Take action. Create. Do something. Apply what you have learned. You can only learn so much in your life. If you don't have a way to release it, it's as good as nothing.

A few great books that can read to fuel your creativity: *Born to Create* by Theresa Dedmon and *Called to Create* by Jordan Raynor.

Listed below are some key ways you can unleash creativity:
- Paint / Draw / Sketch

- Write
- Cook
- Perform
- Take more museum trips

If you want to inspire the world, first inspire yourself.
- Scooter Braun

---

4. Nurture your Mind and Body
- Be mindful
- Take time to understand your strengths and your weaknesses
- Take care of your health.
- Drink lots of water
- Understand the importance of sleep
- Be active
- Be mindful of what you eat
    Holistic health practitioner Ann Wigmore said, "The food you eat can be either the safest and most powerful form of medicine or the slowest form of poison."
- Give yourself a break. Take time to reflect, assess where you at and where you really want to go and don't feel guilty about doing so!

5. Take care of your finances.

Billionaire Warren Buffett's only two rules for investing:

"Rule No. 1: Never lose money. Rule No. 2: Never forget rule No. 1."

Sometimes, others can make us feel guilty for not lending them money. Especially when we hear stories that captivate our hearts, with the end goal of borrowing the money and no plan to pay it back. The thing is, you also have your own life to deal with.

It is important to remember, that most of the time, you are not doing them a favor by lending them what you have. There may be exceptional cases where it is the right thing to do, but the majority of the time, we need to teach them how to fish instead of giving them one.

Take charge of your finances. Listed below are some key ways you can get control of your finances:

- Know where your money is going
- Build an emergency fund
- Learn about investing (real estate, the stock market, commodities, or anything that will work for you) and do it!

Great article about different systems on how to get started:

- https://www.thebalance.com/manage-your-personal-finances-2385812
- https://www.success.com/rohn-5-money-principles-you-need-to-know/

The small things you do today can make a huge difference in

your life, your kids' lives, and the next generation of your family. You can lose all your money, your job, your business, or your circumstances can change, but the skills you've gained when you invested in yourself, no one can take away from you.

Investing in Yourself can earn you returns that will last you for a lifetime. It makes a difference in your life, your well-being, and your ability to thrive and perform to the best of your ability. It doesn't only benefit you; it also attracts and inspires others around you.

If I still didn't convince you to invest in yourself, I'll end this chapter with a quote that may help:

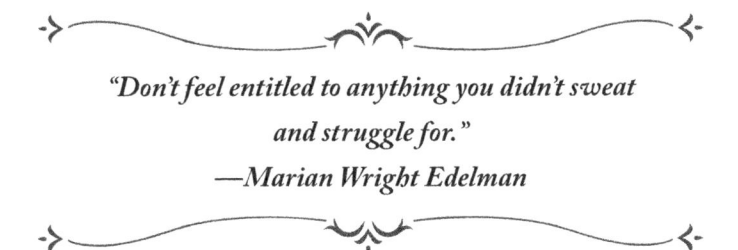

"Don't feel entitled to anything you didn't sweat and struggle for."
—Marian Wright Edelman

CONCLUSION

When I think back to how this all began, one thing is clear for sure: I was clueless from the start what tomorrow would bring, but I wanted a better life.

Looking back at those moments, I didn't realize how difficult it has been. I focused on one thing, to progress in life and not stay where I was. Each step I took eventually brought me to a better life and more than I could imagine. For each small investment I made in myself, I gained a hundred times back.

I believe that you have your own story to tell. You may be in a situation right now where you think it's impossible, or you don't know what to do next. You may not like the direction of your life right now, but the good thing is, it isn't over yet. You are still alive! It's not too late to change.

I hope you will be encouraged and inspired by this book and with the stories I've shared. This is only the first step. What you do with what you learn makes the difference, not only in your life but also with the people around you.

Remember this: It all starts within You.
No matter how tough it is, how dark the place is you're at, there

is another way to live. Don't just survive, be bold and thrive. You decide if it happens. You need to take one step forward every day to get closer to the person you want to be.

Will you allow yourself to be carried away by the flow of your daily routine? Will you look at your circumstances as limitations? If you feel that you do not have the time, money, or resources to make things happen, that is your choice, your decision.

It is limitless where you can go and what you can accomplish. It may not be an immediate change, but with the right mindset, consistency, and having a system in place, you will eventually get there.

We only have one life to live. The question is, will you make the most out of it?
Don't be afraid to take a risk, to change things, to fail. Don't be scared to pursue your dreams. If you know what matters most to you, failure will not stop you from becoming what you want to be.

What's the worst thing that can happen? Fail and get up again. If you're going to fail, fail fast, learn from it and move on. As you take one step, you will realize it is never as scary as it looks.

Stop being a victim and start being the Creator of your life. Wherever you are at…even if it is a place where you are suffering, there is a lesson you can learn if you will keep an open mind.

Remember, when you are not growing anymore, you are dying.

You can live the life you want to create, and if you haven't started working on it, **now is the time**.

WHAT'S NEXT?

It's now your turn!

Whatever your goals and dreams, if you take one step at a time and commit to the process, you can achieve it.

But you can't do it all by yourself. Join OneStepAtATime community, post questions, and let's encourage one another.

Don't forget to Get Free access to https://www.margediblasio.com/one-step-at-a-time-free-resources-su to your free downloads and resources (documents, templates, and many more).

ACKNOWLEDGMENTS

Writing a book is harder than I thought and more rewarding than I could have ever imagined. None of this would have been possible without the following people:

To my family.
First, my mama, my inspiration. Thank you for always being the person I could turn to during those dark and desperate years. You sustained me in ways that I never knew I needed. You stood by me during every struggle and all my successes. To my papa, thanks for bringing the best out of me. The things that happened in the past allowed me to build resilience and become the person I am now. To my brothers, Noly, Marvin and Melvin: you all drive me crazy, but even if I got to choose, I'd still choose to be with you. You guys inspired me every single day, and my dreams started with the three of you. My awesome husband, Mike. Thank you for your love, patience, and encouragement. I am very grateful that you took the time to read every word of my manuscript with a sharp eye and assisted me with the editing. Thank you for supporting me on those late nights when I was writing. Thank you so much mahal. My lovely daughters, Arwen and Amelia, thank you for inspiring me to write this book. Having you both, provided me with a fuller and richer perspective on life. To my mother in law, Elsie: for your loving memory. You inspired me to

write this book. To my father and brother in law: thank you for your love and support.

To all my loving friends and community.
Thank you for supporting, listening and encouraging me.
Special thanks to GJ Gonzales, my mentor, for the friendship and encouragement from the time we first met up to now. Mae Flores, Sheryl Caseres, Lorein Francisco, Jenn Rivera, Claire Moreno and many more, their friendships have been proven over the year. I value you more than I could ever put into words. Mae and Marlon Dy, thanks for sharing your entrepreneurial journey and words of wisdom to pursue my passion. Marina Bershma, thanks for your company and encouragement to keep writing during those times I felt overwhelmed. K Villaroya, who provided some developmental feedback for my manuscript earlier on.

To my naturopath, Dr. Amanda Cressman, who supported me in my health, and helped me to be in my best shape. It made a huge difference in completing this book.

To Rebeca Freeman, who provided her insight and editorial expertise.

To you, dear reader, thanks for investing your time in my book.

Thanks to the many teachers and mentors who have shared their wisdom through books, audios, videos and other online resources.

To the CHC Filipino Community in Singapore. Being involved

in this group was the best and most transformational experience I had. I am very grateful to have this opportunity earlier in my life.

I'd also like to thank the Self Publishing Book (SPS) community, who encouraged and helped me to pursue my dream of writing my story into reality. Special thanks to my coach, Ramy Vance, for helping me find the clarity I needed to write this book and for guiding me in my journey.

It is because of all of you that I have a legacy to pass on to my family where one didn't exist before.

ABOUT THE AUTHOR

Marge is a real estate investor, writer, youth leader, coach, wife, mother, daughter, sister, friend, and a lifelong learner.

Known for her authenticity, genuineness, tech-savviness and engaging presence, Marge specializes in leadership, technology, and creativity. While working as an I.T Professional, and pregnant with her second child, she obtained her real estate license and John Maxwell Team coaching certification in 2016. Later, during her parental leave, she became a certified Realtor. In February 2019, she wrote this book to encourage a wider audience going through dark times. Her journey became a guide to achieve a better life despite life's circumstances. She is passionate about sharing her life experiences and bring out the best in others.

Marge was born in the Philippines, lived in Singapore for three years and is now a long time resident in Ontario, Canada. When not working or writing, she enjoys reading, exercising, painting, traveling, and spending time with her loving husband and two beautiful daughters.

https://margediblasio.com
https://www.johncmaxwellgroup.com/margediblasio
https://investinabetteryou.com/

One More Thing

Thank You for Reading My Book!

This is the book I wish I could have read during the first few years of my journey. If you know someone that could benefit from this book, can you please share it?

Also, I would love to hear what you think. Could you please take a moment to review it on Amazon? Search for One Step At A Time Book Marge Di Blasio. Then leave your feedback.

This can help others to learn how they can benefit from this book. It would also help me understand how I can better serve you, as my dear reader. I can't wait to connect with you!

Manny thanks,
Marge

NOTES

Chapter 1 Dare to Dream
John Maxwell. Your Road Map For Success. Page 25
John Maxwell, Put Your Dream to the Test

Chapter 2 Find your Burning Desire
Simon Sinek. Start With Why. Page 136

Chapter 3 Decisions
Ameet Ranadive, "The Power of Starting with Why", Medium.com, May 26, 2017, https://medium.com/leadership-motivation-and-impact/the-power-of-starting-with-why-f8e491392ef8

Chapter 4
Rania Naim, "There's A Reason Why God Brings You Closer To Certain People And Then Lets Them Go", ThoughtCatalog.com, May 25, 2019
https://thoughtcatalog.com/rania-naim/2018/01/theres-a-reason-why-god-brings-you-closer-to-certain-people-and-then-lets-them-go/

Chapter 5 Delay is not Denial
"26 Affirmations for disappointment, unmet expectations, and delayed answers to prayer" www.thecoffeybreak.com, March 13,

2018, https://www.thecoffeybreak.com/blog-2/2018/3/13/26-affirmations-for-disappointment-unmet-expectations-and-delayed-answers-to-prayer

Chapter 7 Forgiveness
Nancy Colier, "What Is Forgiveness, Really?" Psyhchologytoday.com, Mar 15, 2018
https://www.psychologytoday.com/ca/blog/inviting-monkey-tea/201803/what-is-forgiveness-really

Rose Sweet, "Forgiveness and Restoration", FocusOnTheFamily.com, https://www.focusonthefamily.com/marriage/divorce-and-infidelity/forgiveness-and-restoration/forgiveness-what-it-is-and-what-it-isnt

Chapter 9
Ecclesiastes 3:1-8 New International Version (NIV)

Chapter 10
Christian Smith. The Paradox of Generosity:Giving We Receive, Grasping We Lose

Chapter 11
John Maxwell. Your Road Map For Success

Tara Jacobsen, "5 DIFFERENT GOAL SETTING SYSTEMS… WHICH ONE WORKS FOR YOU?" marketingartfully.com, December 11, 2017 https://marketingartfully.com/5-goal-setting-systems/

Chapter 12 Invest In Yourself
John Maxwell. Your Road Map For Success. Page 107
Marie Forleo, Make Every Man Want You: How to Be so Irresistible You'll Barely Keep from Dating Yourself Marie Forleo. Page XXV

"What is Self-Awareness and How to develop it?", DevelopGoodHabits.com, January 12, 2019, https://www.developgoodhabits.com/what-is-self-awareness/

"The importance of saying No", CoachingPositivePerformance.com, https://www.coachingpositiveperformance.com/the-importance-of-saying-no/

Richard Feloni, "Tony Robbins started out as a broke janitor — then he saved a week's worth of pay, and the way he spent it changed his life", BusinessInsider.com, October 4, 2017 https://www.businessinsider.com/tony-robbins-changed-his-life-at-17-years-old-2017-10

Zameena Mejia, "Warren Buffett says this one investment supersedes all others", CNBC.com, October 4, 2017 https://www.cnbc.com/2017/10/04/warren-buffett-says-this-one-investment-supersedes-all-others.html

"Health Benefits of Creativity" relaxtheback.com, November 26, 2018 https://relaxtheback.com/blogs/news/health-benefits-of-creativity

Royale Scuderi, "3 Valuable Ways to Invest in Yourself", Lifehack.org, https://www.lifehack.org/articles/lifestyle/3-valuable-ways-to-invest-in-yourself.html

Miriam Caldwell, "5 Keys to Successfully Managing Your Personal Finances", TheBalance.com, January 26, 2019, https://www.thebalance.com/manage-your-personal-finances-2385812

"Rohn: 5 Money Principles You Need to Know". Success.com, July 10, 2016
https://www.success.com/rohn-5-money-principles-you-need-to-know/

My Inspirational Resources

Want to accelerate your growth? Read on!
- The Seasons of Life: Jim Rohn
- As Man Thinketh - James Allen
- Think Grow Rich - Napoleon Hill
- Rich Dad Poor Dad – Robert Kiyosaki
- It's Rising Time - Kim Kiyosaki
- Rich Woman - Kim Kiyosaki
- Lean In - Sheryl Sandberg
- Option B – Sheryl Sandberg and Adam Grant
- The Promise of A Pencil
- The 7th Habits of Highly Effective People
- The 8th Habits
- The Power of TED* (*The Empowerment Dynamic): David Emerald
- One Thing I knew For Sure – Oprah Winfrey
- Faith – Phil Pringle
- Soar – T.D Jakes
- The Power of Intention Dr Wayne Dyer
- Living Forward: A Proven Plan to stop drifting and get the life you want – Michael Hyatt and Daniel Harkavy
- What If It Does Work Out: How A Side Hustle Can change your Life – Susie Moore
- Start With Why Simon Sinek
- High Performance Habits: Brendon Burchard
- Make Every Man Want You: How to Be so Irresistible You'll Barely Keep from Dating Yourself Marie Forleo

Made in the
USA
Monee, IL